ADAM THE GARDENER

Adam The Gardener

Cyril Cowell & Morley Adams

Chatto & Windus
LONDON

Published by Chatto & Windus 2011

2 4 6 8 10 9 7 5 3 1

Published in Great Britain in 2011 by
Chatto & Windus
Random House, 20 Vauxhall Bridge Road,
London SW1V 2SA
www.rbooks.co.uk

Addresses for companies within The Random House Group Limited can be found at: www.randomhouse.co.uk/offices.htm

The Random House Group Limited Reg. No. 954009

A CIP catalogue record for this book
is available from the British Library

ISBN 9780701184346

The Random House Group Limited supports The Forest Stewardship Council (FSC), the leading international forest
certification organisation. All our titles that are printed on Greenpeace approved FSC certified paper carry the FSC logo.
Our paper procurement policy can be found at www.rbooks.co.uk/environment

Typeset by Palimpsest Book Production Limited, Falkirk, Stirlingshire
Printed and bound in Great Britain by MPG Books Ltd, Bodmin, Cornwall

INTRODUCTION

by Alys Fowler, 2011

ADAM THE GARDENER **is possibly the grumpiest old man in gardening. Every now and again, however, he lets his guise drop. He looks positively happy about tending his tomatoes in the third week of July and, come October, covering his endives to blanch them almost makes him grin. But mostly he's just grumpy. That's OK; he's an old man gardening.**

Or perhaps Cyril Cowell and Morley Adams didn't want us to concentrate too much on Adam. The joys of the drawings in this book are in the corners, those little detailed boxes that show you just how to layer carnations or graft a cactus. Actually, let's just think about that for a second – grafting a cactus isn't exactly an everyday job for an everyday gardener. The range of work Adam undertakes here is fairly astonishing. He's cooking, bottling, making window boxes, turning compost, picking flowers, growing wonderful cabbages or – my new favourite – blanching dandelion leaves. He's a studious gardener, much like the artist and author must have been. In an amazingly short space Cowell, the artist, and Adams, the genius behind the gardening, manage to draw out a lifetime's worth of knowledge. And here it is, in a wonderful reproduction and ready to be passed on again.

And yes, some of their ideas do seem a little dated. I'm not sure I'd want napthalene on my compost to rid me of slugs (we now know that they're actually doing a good job there), but I love tips like cutting back your broad beans in August to get a second crop of small beans, or using green manures instead of hard-to-source animal ones. If you're tackling a much neglected allotment, head straight to the first week of December to find out exactly how you should go about making your plot workable once more (and he's right about how to hold the spade – you'll dig far more efficiently if you follow his methods). If you ever needed the text-book definition of how to compost, here it is. In the second week of October Adam tackles his compost with exquisite care, beautifully documenting each layer. You can omit the sulphate of ammonia these days, but the waste hair (I'd like to imagine it's his beard trimmings), carpet sweepings and compostable dustbin waste are all spot on and, as he says, you'll soon have 'a constant source of home-made manure'. And if you're stuck for design ideas check out the retro garden-design options towards the back of the book . . .

There's inspiration on every page, so don't skip the bits you think you already know. We've lost a lot of detail about growing over the years. I guess when you have a supermarket full of cheap vegetables, making your broad beans resprout or getting more from your turnip tops just seems like too much effort. But these truly are the hidden gems of this book. Replanting your turnip tops in the fourth week of September and growing them in a warm dark place (Adam has a shed in mind, naturally) is a genius idea and results in these wonderful, sweet, cabbage-flavoured leaves. Thank you, Adam!

There's an assumption that vegetable growing back then was all about producing giant vegetables that would be boiled to death in the kitchen, but this book suggests otherwise. It seems Adam (or Cyril or Morley) was a secret epicure – how else do you explain the second week of August when you get tips on the best flowers for salads and what to do with nasturtium seeds? And did you know that it is wasteful to let perpetual spinach leaves grow too large, as they'll be no good for cooking? Once you've grown them, Adam comes into his own on storing your vegetables – see his carefully made potato clamps, his underground storage boxes for apples, the touching way he hangs up his marrows or suspends his pears from the beams of his shed. These are all tricks we need to relearn.

Adam and his creators were men who didn't waste anything. From radish tops to picture frames they found a use for absolutely everything and, perhaps surprisingly, because of this their work seems fresh and current today. Adam is a true example of the make-do-and-mend generation. He'll teach you how not to waste space with crops, how to save seeds, to make bonfires which will yield potash, what the best dibber should look like (a flattened end, he's very particular about that). Being self-sufficientish in the summer is easy, but come winter it takes much more work – and it's these thrifty, environmentally friendly (you can only imagine what Adam would make of that term) solutions that we need. As long as you ignore the dubious advice about chemicals, with Adam by your side you'll find yourself at the forefront of environmental gardening.

Adam's advice is simple, his instructions wonderfully easy to follow. Before you know, you'll have quite fallen for him and his waistcoat (though one would have thought he might be rather cold in December) and will find yourself asking, as I so often do, 'Now, what would Adam do?'

ADAM THE GARDENER

by

CYRIL COWELL & MORLEY ADAMS

A Pictorial Guide to Each
Week's Work, with a Full
Gardening Calendar & Plans
for New Gardens

1946

A FOREWORD

by Nathaniel Gubbins

WHEN I left London to live in the country I cherished an illusion about gardeners. I thought of them as hardworking, God-fearing men with the simple hearts and honest eyes of children. I thought that, living as they do, always so near to nature and free of the worry and petty strife of the big cities, their minds would be calm and untroubled and their natures sweet and reasonable.

Since then I have learned a lot about gardeners.

I have found that close association with nature does not make a man love nature. There is nobody who hates gardens more than a gardener.

Nor does the simple, natural life make a man love his fellow-men. There is nobody who hates gardeners more than another gardener.

To a gardener nature is an enemy to be fought and tamed into submission; another gardener is a rival to be sneered at as an incompetent fool.

In fact, gardeners are just like other men who fight for an existence in the big cities, except that the gardener is a shade more vicious, a little more unreasonable, a great deal more childish.

During one of my absent-minded moments I once engaged two gardeners to work in my garden on the same day.

Although they had been friends and neighbours for many years, the sight of each other in my garden turned them into fiends, glaring hatred at each other, muttering curses at each other and even hiding tools from each other.

Their hatred was so intense that it seemed to penetrate into the house, souring the day and getting everybody's nerves on edge. During the afternoon I heard the sound of grunting and heavy breathing beneath my window and was amazed to see these middle-aged children engaged in a grim, wordless, life-and-death struggle for the possession of a spade.

So you can see that the garden is no place where simple honest hearts and sweet natures may be found. It is a place where savage battles with weeds and worms and men are fought and where bitter jealousies rage.

This is why, I think, I am so attached to Adam the Gardener who has been my companion on page 3 of the *Sunday Express* for so many years. Adam is my ideal gardener, the one I dreamed about when I lived in London.

For years I have watched him at work, always doing exactly the right thing at exactly the right time.

You never catch Adam late with his potatoes or runner-beans. You never catch him idling in the tool shed, drinking your tea ration and eating your butter ration.

There he is, winter and summer, spring and autumn, hard at work with his hoe or rake, or down on his knees weeding or lining up his onions like soldiers on parade and dressing his carrots by the right.

I have even grown to admire his smart, though not too smart, felt hat, always worn at the correct angle, his sturdy legs in corduroys tied neatly below the knee, and his plain, honest face in which there is no hatred, no rancour, in fact no expression of any known human emotion.

And unlike gardeners of flesh and blood he never argues, never complains of rheumatism and never asks for a day off.

When the *Sunday Express* is published on high days and holidays, like Easter Sunday and Whit Sunday, or even when Christmas Day falls on a Sunday, Adam is still there, pottering about and making himself useful instead of making a beast of himself on Christmas cheer, like some gardeners I know.

Nathaniel Gubbins

CONTENTS

PAGE NO.

GLOSSARY OF GARDENING TERMS 5

ARTIFICIAL FERTILISERS 7

GARDEN GADGETS 8

PICTORIAL GUIDE TO GARDENING WORK FOR EVERY WEEK OF THE YEAR 9

PLANNING NEW GARDENS 105

SUGGESTED LAYOUTS FOR BACK GARDENS 107

IDEAS FOR FRONT GARDENS 111

SPRING FLOWER-BEDS 113

MIXED SUMMER BEDS 114

COLOUR HARMONY IN THE GARDEN 115

ADAM'S GARDENING CALENDAR 116

A PAGE OF 'DO'S' 140

A PAGE OF 'DON'TS' 141

THREE TIPS FROM ADAM 142

INDEX 143

A GLOSSARY OF GARDENING TERMS

Annuals Plants which bloom, produce seed and die during the same season.

Hardy Annuals Plants which pass through all stages of growth in open ground, needing no protection. Sown March or April for July and August blooms, or in August for June flowering.

Half-hardy Annuals Plants which, in their early stages of growth, need artificial heat; later they are planted out in the open for flowering and seed ripening. Sown in heated greenhouse or frame in January, February or March. Seedlings planted out of doors in May for summer blooming.

Biennials Plants which need two seasons to arrive at full maturity. Sown in the open on reserve border in May or June; plants are set out in flowering quarters in autumn.

Perennials or Herbaceous Plants Plants which continue to live and increase in the open for several years. Stems die down each season and grow up again from the roots each spring. Sow in greenhouse in March or in the open in April, May or June.

Spit The length of a spade blade as a measure of depth in digging.

Rod 30¼ square yards.

Suckers   Useless shoots from the stock on which a tree is budded. On rose, plum and lilac, suckers form freely. Sever them at their source. Rose suckers are thorny, usually have seven leaflets of pale colour. A true rose leaf has five leaflets.

Subsoil   The soil lying below that which is cultivated.

Taking the Bud   The removing of superfluous flower-buds on chrysanthemums which form below the first, so that this chief bud may develop.

Tilth   Soil broken down finely to make it suitable for sowing or planting.

Tap-root   Main root of a tree or plant.

Humus   Decayed vegetable matter.

Blind   A plant or shoot which fails to produce flowers or leaves.

Crown   The bud-like centre of strawberry plant or the top of root-stock of hardy herbaceous plants.

Lateral   A secondary shoot which develops on a main branch.

Loam   The top spit of turf decayed, after a year's stacking, into mellow soil.

Mulch   A layer of manure, lawn mowings or other material laid around trees and plants to keep the soil moist.

Offset   Small bulbs attached to parent bulbs or small rooted pieces of hardy plants. In each case they are detached for propagation.

ARTIFICIAL FERTILISERS

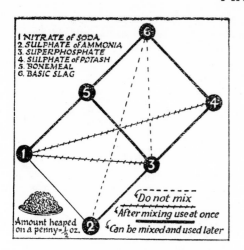

1. NITRATE of SODA
2. SULPHATE of AMMONIA
3. SUPERPHOSPHATE
4. SULPHATE of POTASH
5. BONEMEAL
6. BASIC SLAG

Amount heaped on a penny = ½ oz.

Do not mix
After mixing use at once
Can be mixed and used later

Artificial fertilisers are most useful when natural manures are not available, and as a supplement to vegetable refuse. The six main kinds are numbered here. Nitrogenous manures, 1 and 2, stimulate foliage and roots. Phosphatic manures, 3, 5, and 6, have the opposite effect, checking rampant growth, but promoting fruit and flower growth. Potassic manures, 4, including wood-ash, benefit plants in all stages of growth. Artificials are in concentrated form; only small dressings, such as 1 or 2 ozs. per sq. yard must be applied, and then hoed in. Don't allow them to come in contact with leaves, or they may scorch the plants. Use No. 1 around growing plants only; it dissolves quickly. Nos. 2 and 3 should be used only in ground containing lime; No. 6 is best for soil deficient in lime. When making up artificial fertilisers, remember that although most chemicals can be mixed safely, others should be used at once when mixed, while some should not be mixed at all. The numbers in the diagram refer to those in the first picture. Fertile soil having a good supply of humus will produce good crops on artificials alone for some years, but natural manure is necessary after a period.

A GARDEN LINE

Cut a pair of pointed stakes. On the top of each fit a large cotton or thread reel. One of these is made fast for winding; the other left loose for winding the line, which should be of strong twine.

A PLANTING DIBBER

A dibber for planting bulbs, potatoes, etc., can be made from an old spade-handle. By boring holes at measured points and inserting a wooden pin, as shown, the depth of the hole can be regulated accurately.

7

GARDEN GADGETS

AN ADJUSTABLE DRILL-MAKER

Wing nut →

A home-made drill-maker will save time and work on your plot. A board is needed in which holes are made at various distances apart. The adjustable wooden 'teeth' are fastened to the board by wing-nuts, enabling them to be moved to other holes. The broom-handle fits into a hole in the centre of a block fixed to the board.

AN EARWIG TRAP

Fold small pieces of corrugated cardboard. Insert them into matchbox covers. Tie them to the stakes supporting chrysanthemums, dahlias, etc. Earwigs will shelter in the traps and can be shaken out and killed.

A SEEDLING BED-MARKER

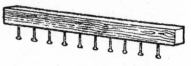

Where a large number of seedlings have to be planted out this bed-marker will save time. Strong wire nails are driven at equal distances into a long strip of wood. With this a number of spaces can be marked out at the same time.

AN ADJUSTABLE TOOL HANDLE

An easily adjustable handle which will fit any tools with a tapered socket can be made by shaping the end of a broom-handle to a long tapering point. Drive a nail into the tip. Twist a length of wire tightly round in a spiral, securing the end. Twist the handle into the tool socket to secure it. To release the handle when needed for another tool twist it in the opposite direction.

A SEED PROTECTOR

Two boards with supporting pegs are each studded on three sides with nails. The boards are set at the ends of the row. Black thread is stretched from end to end of the row, twisting it around the nails. This forms a protecting cover to the seed-bed from birds.

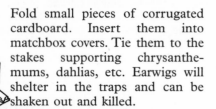

Plants in cold frames can be protected from frost at night by laying sacking or mats over the frames and heaping ashes around the outsides of the frames. Celery, parsnips, turnips and horse-radish should be surrounded with straw. Pairs of boards nailed together and placed over celery plants will keep rain off.

In some districts rose trees suffer damage from cold. Standards which may be treated as shown, are more liable than dwarf trees. Peg down or shorten long shoots of the latter. By being blown about a hole is formed at the stem base, making the soil sodden. Inset (X) shows wirenetting round choice plants to enclose a covering of leaves.

The protection given by artificial heat in greenhouses can be supplemented by placing crumpled sheets of paper over plants. The paper acts in a similar way to clouds over the earth, preventing to a great extent the heat given off by plants from being wasted. Newspapers, spread over plants in the cold greenhouse, will protect them from frost.

By making a hotbed, the cultivation of plants in a frame placed on it will enable you to obtain early supplies of vegetables. Hotbeds can be made of fresh stable manure alone, with dry leaves added, or of leaves alone. The addition of leaves produces a more lasting but less intense heat than one made of manure alone. The manure heap must be turned inside out several times during a week or 10 days and kept covered during that period.

If the heap is too dry moisten it. Then let it stand for a few days. Choose a sheltered spot for the bed, dig out a space about 6 in. deep, 1 ft. longer and wider than the size of your frame. Place a layer of rubble in the bottom and, when the heap is ready, begin building up your bed, keeping it together as shown. Tread each layer of manure or leaves fairly firmly, putting aside any strawy material for the outer covering of the bed.

When completed, the bed should be 2 ft. or 3 ft. high. The frame, when placed in position, is filled 6 in. deep with good sifted soil and leaf-mould. This will make a fine seed-bed when levelled. When the heat generated has fallen to about 75 degrees, which should be a week later, the seed-bed is ready. In the spring the gardener will find it useful for raising cucumbers, vegetable marrows, celery and half-hardy annuals.

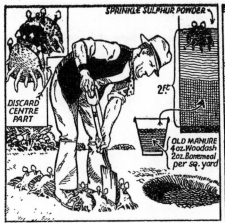

Dig a trench around clumps of rhubarb which have not been moved and divided for three or more years. The trench will help to avoid injury to roots when lifting the 'stools.' Ease each out with a fork and cut each into three pieces with a sharp spade. The centre piece, the oldest, is discarded; the others should each contain two crowns. Dig 2 ft. deep on a fresh site on which to replant these 3 ft. apart. With each square yard of soil mix ¾ bucketful of rotted manure, 4 oz. wood ashes and 2 oz. bonemeal.

The tips of the crowns only must be left uncovered when replanting. Good clumps can be forced into growth for early use by lifting now, and, after leaving exposed to frost for a few days, placing them under the greenhouse staging. Pack soil tightly around each. Over this put a thick layer of leaves. Place boards against the staging uprights to prevent soil and leaves falling out. Water well and hang sacking from staging to floor to keep roots in darkness.

Rhubarb clumps can also be forced where they are growing by covering them with bottomless tubs, boxes or pots. Over the cover heap some decayed leaves, manure, old grass cuttings or straw. If a few roots are covered in this way every few weeks a supply can be constantly maintained. These roots will not be ready quite so early as those forced under glass. Sulphur powder sprinkled in planting holes and over roots will prevent disease.

Constant watch must be kept on the plot for pests. Some are soil pests, found mostly below the surface. The wireworm and cutworm are two of the worst offenders. The first, as its name implies, is wiry and wormlike of light brown colour. Check by liming, but to each 7 lb. mix 1 lb. naphthalene. Potatoes, turnips or carrots skewered on sticks or wire can be buried, leaving tops of skewers visible. A weekly inspection of these traps will enable you to kill any pests found feeding on the bait.

Cutworms are dull, grey-green caterpillars; they can be destroyed by a *poison* bait, made by mixing dry Paris green, 1 part, with 24 parts coarse bran. When using, damp it slightly. Wash hands after, owing to its poisonous nature. Millipedes, which coil themselves, are dark grey. Trap or poison them similarly to other soil pests. Slugs can be checked by liming soil. Small heaps of bran, covered by pots, will trap them. The poison bait is also effective.

Snails are best collected by hand and dropped in a strong solution of salt and water. Woodlice are trapped by hollowed pieces of apple or potato. Cabbage White Butterfly caterpillars do great damage during the hearting stage to all plants of the cabbage family. They are fat, yellow, with dark spots. Hand-pick them, and spray plants with one tablespoon salt to one gallon water, or use ammonia water.

In a heated greenhouse the seeds of gloxinia, mixed or separate colours, may be sown. Seed boxes filled with finest compost should be immersed in tepid water. After the surplus water has drained sow the seeds thinly, sprinkling a little fine silver sand among them, and putting a pane of glass over the boxes. Expose them to light.

Other seeds to sow in boxes now are tuberous begonia, verbena, canna and streptocarpus, or Cape primrose. Loosen the soil around roses with a fork, and apply 2 oz. per square yard of basic slag. Give a top dressing of peat and leaf-mould to rhododendrons and azaleas. Other shrubs need manure and leaf-mould dug in around them.

Wallflowers which are becoming 'leggy' should have their tips pinched out. In suitable weather Canterbury bells, wallflowers, evening primrose, sweet-williams, and other early spring flowering plants may be transplanted. Thorough weeding now will save work later. Keep an eye open for slugs and snails in the rockery, and destroy.

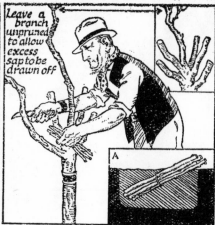

Winter pruning may be done while fruit trees are dormant until March. Cut back all side shoots, except natural fruit spurs, to within three or four buds of their bases, cutting just above an outwardly pointing bud to form fruit spurs. Shorten over-crowded fruit spurs on old trees. Cut back terminal or leader shoots at the ends of main branches to within 9 in. or 1 ft. of their bases, usually one-third or half their length. Remove crowded growths, keeping main branches evenly spaced to allow light and air to have access to ripen fruit.

Cut back now main branches of any trees you intend to top graft in spring. These are cut to within 2 ft. of trunk, but leave one unpruned to act as safety valve so that excess sap can be drawn off. Select healthy growths while pruning now for use as the grafts. These are tied in bundles, laid in a north-facing trench, and covered two-thirds their length (inset A). This keeps them alive but inactive, retarding them until grafting time.

Any big pruning cuts or rotted parts cut away should be sealed over with white lead paint to prevent disease entering. See that the grease bands are renewed where needed. Scrape away any dead leaves or other material adhering to them. Spray fruit trees with a tar winter wash to destroy pests, such as apple suckers, after pruning, on a dry, windless day, when not freezing. Give fruit trees a manure mulch next month.

It is not essential to use expensive rocks for constructing a rock garden; broken concrete, irregularly shaped slabs of stone, pounded mortar rubble, and old brick will do. Before building the rockery excavate the soil 2 ft. deep, place a layer of clinkers over the bottom, above which put inverted turves, and when replacing the soil mix with it some rotted leaf-mould and a good quantity of coarse sand.

The site chosen should be open and away from overhanging trees. Design your rockery so that some parts are above and others below the normal ground level. In laying the stones see that each is placed with an inward and downward slope so that moisture may penetrate to the centre of the mound. A winding path of limestone chippings giving access to all parts of the rockery is best.

Porous material is better than very hard stones such as quartz or granite. When planting, use small, fresh young pieces, each with roots, rather than large clumps. They should be firmly planted, care being taken that the roots will be able to reach the deeper soil, giving ample space for each small plant to develop. Leave no air spaces for the roots of the plants to creep into, or they will suffer in dry weather.

To provide a crop of early peas the ground should be prepared now by opening trenches 1 ft. wide, running north and south. Excavate the soil 2 ft. deep, placing the upper soil on one side of the trench and the lower on the other. The soil must be fairly rich. It must not dry out in hot weather. Break up bottom of trench to a depth of 6 in., placing on it a 3 in. layer of decayed manure.

When replacing lower spit, well broken up, mix with it a pailful of littery manure per yard run of trench, or straw cut into short lengths, and 2 oz. crushed bones. Press down soil before returning top soil, with which rotted manure at the rate of one pailful per yard run, 4 oz. wood ashes and 1 oz. bonemeal are mixed. Leave top soil rough, scattering lime on surface and forking in lightly.

Sow early lettuce on a border facing south which has been dug and manured. Rake surface fine, smooth and level, and if not manured for a previous crop give a dressing of ground hoof, 2 oz. per yard, forking it in, or at the same rate use three parts bonemeal, two parts superphosphate and plenty of wood ash. Soak seed in water an hour before sowing. Sow thinly in ½-in. deep drills, 6 in. apart. Run a line of fine cinders along each side of row to avoid slugs. A dressing of hydrated lime, 1 oz. per square yard, is beneficial.

To start begonia and gloxinia tubers into growth you need boxes not less than 3 in. deep. These are filled with fibre or leafy soil, and the tubers are set 1 in. apart, light soil being sprinkled between them, leaving the tops uncovered. When rooted, they are potted separately in small pots. Temperature before rooting, 60 degrees; afterwards 50–55.

Bedding plants can be propagated by taking cuttings from those which were potted in autumn and wintered in the greenhouse. Autumn-rooted cuttings should be potted separately now. Cuttings of zonal geraniums or pelargoniums, taken just below a joint, potted separately when rooted, and placed in a cold frame, all blooms being picked off, will flower in the greenhouse during winter.

Prune fuchsias which have been stored during winter, shortening the branches by half. When top-dressed as shown, water and place in a warm corner of the greenhouse. Shoots will form, which, when 3 in. long, may be taken off with 'heel,' lower leaves trimmed off, and the cuttings inserted deeply round edges of pots. Plunge pots in fibre-filled box covered with glass. Pot singly in small pots after a week.

a = Decayed Garden Refuse.
b = Decayed Manure.
c = Top Soil.
d = Soot, wood ash, bonemeal.

1 part Sand
1 part Leaf-mould
3 parts Loam

+ 1 oz. Soot per bucketful

leaves compost sifted soil

STRAW or BUSHY STICKS
FINE SOIL and WOOD ASH
6 in.

Varieties:-
for frames:
Little Gem.
Early Horn.
for borders:
Early Gem.
Guerande.
Early—
—Nantes.

A row or two of an early kind of onion, suitable for salads, such as White Lisbon, can be sown now in a bed prepared thoroughly, as shown, in a sunny position. The ground should be trenched deeply, made moderately firm by treading, stones and lumps removed, and the surface made fine and level. The seed for this purpose can be sown fairly thickly in ½-in. deep drills. These spring, or green, onions are pulled in spring when young.

To produce really good-sized onions sow now in boxes of a compost made up similarly to that shown here. This compost should be sterilised by pouring boiling water over it. Space the seeds, using only the larger ones, at ¼ in. apart, pressing them gently into the soil with a board. For covering soil use some from the compost, heating it on a shovel held over a fire. Sift it finely, and sprinkle it over the seeds. When seedlings stand erect, prick them off at 2 in. apart into other boxes.

The first outdoor sowing of early shorthorn kinds of carrot can be made now on a warm border in 1 in. deep drills, 6 in. apart. Cover with fine soil and protect from hard weather with dried bracken, straw or bushy sticks, removing these when seedlings are well through. If soil is in a wet condition delay sowing until it is in a fit state to rake down finely. Sowing can also be made in a cold frame made frostproof at night with sacking.

A sloping bank faced with a retaining wall of stone slabs arranged horizontally forms an ideal place for alpine plants. Between each row of stone there should be a thin layer of soil. As each is placed see that the front edge recedes slightly from that below, so that it will be better able to retain moisture. Pockets should be left here and there to allow for planting. Mix mortar rubble or sand with the soil behind the stones, ramming and packing it firmly. Aubrietia and double white arabis grow vigorously on this type of wall.

Alpines may be grown in pots and pans of various sizes containing a good compost. Wedge pieces of limestone between the small plants. To minimise effects of frost, pots may be plunged to their rims in cinder ashes in a frame, or placed in an unheated greenhouse. To allow for ventilation the lights of frames should be raised on supports 2 in. higher than the back and front of the frame.

If sheets of glass fixed to stakes by wires or spans of two sheets joined by a ridge are put over alpines, shelter from rain will be provided on the rockery. Seeds of alpines sown in pots or pans should be put in a cold frame, the soil used being of porous nature. Peat-loving plants should have peat evenly sprinkled over the pan by rubbing it through a sieve. Should a fall of snow occur, heap it over the seed pans; it will cause quicker germination.

A strawberry bed can be made now. Loamy soil is best, but most soils, if prepared previously, are suitable for planting. Lighten heavy soil, or, if soil is light, put in some turfy loam and hop manure. Give the surface a dressing of basic slag, forking it in lightly. Choose an open but windsheltered position for the bed. Use a trowel when planting. The centre bud or 'crown' should be embedded, but not buried, in the surface soil. Rows are made 2 ft. apart.

Canker on fruit trees may cause blossom, branches, or even a whole tree, if it is young, to die. The signs of canker are crusty swellings, often forming after an attack of woolly aphis. To control this disease, cut out the cankered parts, or, if badly affected, a whole branch must be cut off behind the canker. Small spots are removed by paring away the diseased tissue and then sealing the wounds over with lead paint.

This is a good time in which to give your fruit bushes and trees a good stimulating feed. They will produce better fruit. Superphosphate, sulphate of ammonia, and a good quantity of wood ashes scattered around the trees makes a suitable dressing. Hoe soil after applying, and follow up with a mulch of old manure, not letting this come into contact with the trees.

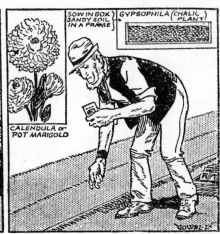

Prepare deep, rich soil as shown, and sow seeds of sweet peas out of doors. Allow 3 ft. between the rows and 3 in. between the seeds, which are placed 1 in. deep. Chip hard-skinned seeds with a knife, taking care not to injure the germ; this will help germination. Protect from birds by a network of stretched black thread. Later, tree twigs can be placed between the plants to help them to stand upright and still give protection from birds.

Among seeds which can now be sown in pots, pans or boxes, filled with a compost similar to that shown, are *Phlox drummondii*, salpiglossis, carnation, ten-week stock, lobelia, petunia, tobacco flower, kochia and canna. Place in a greenhouse with a temperature of 50 degrees. Cuttings which have been in small pots or boxes throughout the winter, such as zonal pelargoniums, begin to make growth, and should be repotted into larger pots.

Sow calendula out of doors in a sunny position in rows about 1 ft. apart, covering the seeds with a sprinkling of soil. Thin the seedlings, when about 1 in. high, to 1 ft. apart. In the vegetable garden parsnip, broad bean, spinach and early peas can be sown now. Place seed potatoes in shallow trays, rose end upwards, in a frost-proof place fully open to the light. Then by planting time the tubers will possess several short sturdy sprouts.

GREEN PEAS

A. Bottom of 2 ft. deep trench forked

B. 3 in. layer manure

C. Subsoil, manure & crushed bones.

D. Topsoil, manure, woodash & bonemeal

Trench dug 20 in. deep

1 ft. ½

Lower soil replaced mixed with decayed garden refuse and hop manure

LEEKS

A. Bottom of trench forked adding vegetable refuse

B. 3 in. layer, old manure

C. Rough leaves mixed with bottom spit.

D. Old manure, Leafmould Bonemeal, with top spit

Soot

CELERY

COWELL

To obtain a successful crop of green peas the site should be prepared well in advance of sowing. Take out a trench 1 ft. wide, 2 ft. deep, placing the bottom layer on one side of the trench and the top on the other. Fork soil at the bottom 6 in. deep. On this lay manure or chopped straw. Break up subsoil as you return it, mixing with it a bucketful of strawy manure to each yard run and 2 oz. crushed bones. When returning top soil mix old manure, 4 oz. wood ash and 1 oz. bonemeal with each yard run.

It pays to prepare ground for leeks thoroughly. Dig a trench 20 in. deep, 1½ ft. wide, keeping layers separate. Fork trench one more foot, working in material from compost heap; this can also be added to hop manure when returning subsoil. Prepare site now; it will then be in condition when the time comes for planting out seedlings. Last year's pea or potato plot would be suitable for leeks.

Prepare celery trenches to ensure soil having a long mellowing. Make two or more trenches 15 in. wide, 2 ft. apart, prepared as shown. These will each take a double staggered row of plants. Mix one-third barrowful of leaves to each barrowful of subsoil. With top soil mix one-third barrowful each of old manure and leaf-mould to each barrow of soil, and two handfuls of bonemeal. Fill trench to within 3 in. of top, leaving a surplus to form a bank between trenches. Sprinkle soot on surface.

When the fronds of ferns start to uncurl, repotting should be done if the ferns are too large for their pots. Cut off faded fronds, the parts as shown, and put into larger pots filled with a compost of equal parts loam, leaf-mould and peat, with silver sand and pieces of charcoal mixed in. This is the time to repot hothouse ferns. Greenhouse ferns should be done in March and room ferns in April.

Divide large ferns into pieces and pot these separately. To propagate by spores, suspend a frond in a paper bag; the tiny ripe spores will drop to the bottom in a few hours. Sow these on surface of compost in pots or seed-pans covered with glass. Allow them to stand in water in a warm green-house. The house atmosphere where ferns are grown must always be kept moist by damping the floor and staging at frequent intervals.

From the spore grows the prothallus. When these are ¼ in. high they are pricked out in pots. The young ferns which develop from the prothallia are potted singly. Some ferns produce bulbils at the ends of their fronds. Peg these down in a pot, and, when rooted, cut away. Shade is essential to ferns from the beginning, and if left in bright sunshine in the summer they will suffer, unless syringed at midday.

A succession of bloom can be obtained from July to mid-September by sowing corms of gladioli at fortnightly intervals from now till the end of April. Place the corms in fibre before planting to make them swell out. Prepare the soil beforehand, choosing warm, open sites. The small-flowered or G. *primulinus* are set 6 in. apart, covered with 2 to 3 in. of soil.

The large-flowered kinds are set 8 in. apart at the same depth. When planting in groups dig a hole of correct depth and set the corms on sand. When planting in separate holes use a trowel, not a dibber. Give surface a dressing of basic slag. A row on a spare border will provide a supply of cutting flowers. Fix stakes, joining string before planting.

Place old stored dahlia roots in deep boxes, lightly covering them with a leafy soil, in warmth; syringe once a day. New shoots, when 3 in. high, are cut off with a small piece of tuber attached. Insert these in pots of sifted sandy loam, cover with glass, and when rooted in a few weeks' time repot in 4-in. pots. Have some labels ready to write name and type on for new pots.

If the roots of any pot-plants are visible from the drainage hole, they should be repotted into slightly larger pots; these and the crocks to be used as drainage must be thoroughly scrubbed and dried beforehand. Use hot water containing a little soft soap. New pots should be soaked in water for some hours before use. A thin strip of paper placed between each pot when storing will prevent them adhering one to another.

An oyster-shell or curved piece of crock is placed, hollow side downward, over the pot-hole, and other broken crocks laid as shown. Use small pieces for hard-wooded subjects and larger pieces for softwooded plants, such as geraniums. Over these put a layer of chopped turf or leaves, etc., to prevent loose compost from dropping among the crocks. Proportions of ingredients for use as compost are shown; these may be slightly varied.

Spread the plant upside down on fingers of one hand, rap rim of old pot gently, lift pot clear, remove old crocks, make few inches of soil in new pot firm, place plant complete with root-ball in, work round and ram firm compost, leaving space at top for watering. A potting bench with sections to hold sand, etc., pots, crocks and potting-stick, made from an old broom handle rounded at one end and cut chisel-shaped at the other, is useful.

In an open sunny position shallots can be planted now, conditions being suitable. The site must be in deeply cultivated soil enriched with manure. Poorly prepared ground produces small bulbs. Use a trowel when planting the bulbs, making a hole for each. Only half bury the bulbs, pressing the soil lightly around them. Eight inches should separate the bulbs in the rows, which are made 1 ft. apart.

Where ground was manured some time ago the planting of early potatoes only necessitates forking it 1 ft. deep, then firming it, making the drills 5 in. deep. On an uncultivated plot, digging 2 ft. deep must be done. Then make 9-in. deep drills, placing a 4-in. layer of manure along the bottom. On this sprinkle leaf-mould or grass cuttings. Set the tubers 9 in. apart, rose end uppermost. Drills should be about 18 in. apart.

Young seedlings, especially peas, need protection from birds. Wire guards form such protection. A rough framework (as in inset A), placed at each end of a row, with lines of black thread stretched between them, makes a good substitute. As a protection from severe weather, place boards along each side of a row, with a covering of glass (as in B). Autumn-sown peas, spring cabbages and broad beans need earthing up and the hoe kept in use.

The first sowings of salad crops can now be made in suitable weather. Don't sow too much at a time; regular fortnightly sowings using just sufficient seed is more economical. A nursery bed is necessary for lettuce, deeply dug, and leaf-mould worked in in preference to manure. Sow very thinly, covering seed by a light raking. Protect seedlings from birds by a raised netting covering the bed. When seedlings have formed two or three rough leaves they will be ready to be planted out at 9 ins. apart.

For the earliest sowings of radishes choose the hardier long varieties; use the round kinds for later crops. The bed should be forked 1 ft. deep, and with each square yard incorporate about half bucketful of hop manure and 4 oz. wood ashes. Soak seed in paraffin for half an hour to prevent destruction by pests. Avoid waste by thin sowing. Radishes are not transplanted. When seedlings of this sowing are half grown, a further sowing can be made.

Mustard and cress is easily and quickly grown, a continuous supply being assured if fortnightly sowings are made in boxes under glass. Coarser material is placed in a layer at the bottom of the box, the compost reaching to within ½ in. of the top. Sow thickly in separate boxes, cress being sown three days before mustard as it takes slightly longer to grow. After cutting, make successive sowings by replacing top layer of compost with fresh material.

Stone troughs or old kitchen sinks make suitable receptacles in which to make miniature rock gardens. These must have efficient drainage, to obtain which holes must be drilled or cut. See that all the water runs away. In the case of old sinks, it may be found that a hollow depression allows some to settle; an extra hole must be made.

The trough must stand firm, its weight not being allowed to cause any tilting. The outlet holes are covered with drainage crocks, and a layer of crocks placed over the bottom. On these place fibrous turf to a depth of 1½ in. The compost to fill the trough is shown. Flowerpots broken into tiny pieces will make a good form of grit.

Arrange the rocks with care, then fill the spaces with the rest of the soil. Dwarf juniper, willow or yew should be planted. Suitable plants are the saxifrages, dwarf campanulas, rock pinks and primulas; *Miosotis rupicola*, the mountain forget-me-not; sedum, cobweb houseleek and *Silene acaulis*. Kept weeded and watered, it will be of unending interest.

Forced dandelion leaves form a good salad addition, similar to, and perhaps better than, endive; they may also be boiled, and the roasted roots, ground when cold, make a useful substitute for coffee. Get seed from seedsmen; wild dandelion leaves are tough. Sow in rows 1 ft. apart, thinning plants to 1 ft. apart. In late summer lift roots, twist off leaves, and plant roots in bundles in covered boxes of soil in warmth. Keep fairly moist. Blanched leaves are then ready in a fortnight. Plants can also be blanched in the open by covering each with a pot.

American or land cress as a salad plant is sown from April to June, and in autumn for winter salads. Sow in drills 9 in. apart, with slight soil covering in good rich soil in semi-shade. Constant moisture is necessary. At intervals of a few days sow thickly in the open ordinary cress, two or three days earlier than mustard, so that both are ready for use at the same time. Cut the little plants when the mustard is about an inch high. Later, in hot, dry weather it should be grown in a shady place.

Watercress can be cultivated in your garden. Use the large brown-leaved kind. Take out a 2 ft. wide trench, 1 ft. deep, fill in with decayed manure to half the depth, adding 3 in. of soil and finishing with a layer of sand, with which the seed is also lightly covered. Tips of shoots 2 in. long, cut just below a joint, inserted 3 in. apart, is another way of obtaining a crop. Soil must be kept moist. By the way, the true botanical name of watercress is nasturtium, and the flower that is commonly known by that name is really *tropæolum*.

Lilies, such as *pardalinum, speciosum, tigrinum, regale* and *auratum,* can be planted now in deep soil either in sunny or semi-shady positions. Hot, dry conditions are not suitable. A hole, 2 ft. wide by the same depth, filled with a compost as shown will take a group of five bulbs. Both *auratum* and *pardalinum* lilies dislike lime; the last mentioned does well amongst rhododendrons.

Set the bulbs 5 in. deep, 9 in. apart, in a slanting position so that moisture will not collect in their scales. Those named, with the exception of *auratum,* can remain undisturbed for some years. They increase in size as they get older; *auratum* usually deteriorates after the first year. Top-dress with well-rotted manure in May or June.

These lilies may also be grown singly in 8-in. pots filled to one-third of their depth with the moistened compost shown. Set bulbs on a layer of sand, and fill remaining space with coconut fibre, which replace with soil in six weeks when growth has started. If no artificial warmth is given, protect from frost.

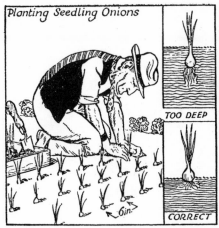

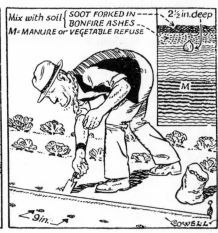

When seedling onions are well rooted harden off in a cold frame. They can then be planted out of doors this month on a prepared bed. Set them 6 in. apart in rows 10 in. or 1 ft. apart. Do not plant too deeply or thick-necked onions which do not keep well will result. The little bulbs should merely rest on, or be only partly covered by, soil. Keep the soil alongside the bulbs quite firm, but between the rows it should be kept loose by light pricking with the fork, care being taken not to work too near the plants. Weed between the rows by hand when soil is damp.

Applications of nitrate of soda or sulphate of ammonia will stimulate growth and so help to keep the destructive onion fly away. Soot dusted over the plants frequently will greatly benefit them. The main crop of onions may be sown now on a bed prepared by deep digging, incorporating manure or garden refuse with the lower spit and wood ashes and soot with the upper part. The surface must be made very fine and firm. Sow seed thinly in ½-in. deep drills, 1 ft. apart, covering them by lightly passing the rake over. Keep down the weeds with the hoe later.

Onion sets, raised from seed sown last summer, are not so liable to be attacked by the onion fly. Some may run to seed, but most will produce onions of medium size. They are planted about 2½ in. deep from the top of the bulb to the surface soil. Shallow planting may tend to cause them to bolt. Prepare the bed as carefully as, and similarly to, that for seeds, making the surface firm. Set the bulbs about 9 in. apart, but less than this distance will be safe if space is limited.

Start your rose-pruning now. To obtain few but good quality blooms, the pruning should be severe; light pruning will produce many blooms of medium quality. Remove all overcrowded weak shoots and dead wood, using a good knife or secateurs. While pruning, keep the centre of the tree clear and the shape well proportioned. Cut out the weakest of two shoots crossing each other.

The weakest of those shoots retained should be cut back to leave about three 'eyes' or buds; the more vigorous shoots may have six or eight left. Always cut down to a bud pointing outwards. The cuts should be clean and sloping, as shown; avoid the faults seen in the insets. Do not allow suckers to grow; cut them out at once or they will kill the plant.

Pruning should begin with hybrid perpetuals, the hybrid tea and pernetiana roses being left for a few weeks. The strength of a bloom is in proportion to the shoot on which it is growing, the strength of the shoot depending on how low it starts. Bush roses produce blooms from shoots of the current year; leave some separated main branches, shortening them by about half.

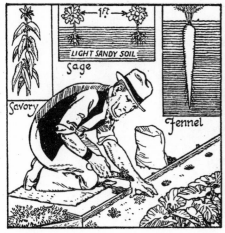

The main use to which herbs are put is the flavouring of salads, soups and stews, but they are also valuable to a certain extent in safeguarding nearby plants from insect attacks. They may be grown as an edging, in a separate bed, or intercropped among other vegetables. Most herbs are not particular as to soil, but a light sandy, well-drained one in a sunny position is best for most kinds.

Savory, a hardy herb, is sown now in drills 1 ft. apart. Pull up when coming into flower, tie in bundles, hang until dry, and store leaves in air-tight bottles. Sage: sow now or raise from cuttings; thin to 1 ft. Fennel: flavours fish sauces; plant tap root 1 in. below surface; see that it can grow straight down. Thyme: sow now, or plant divisions 9 in. apart; give 2 oz. per square yard dressing of lime.

Parsley: sow thinly and thin plants to 6 in. apart. Tarragon: leaves used fresh in salads or dried for seasoning; plant roots 6 in. apart; line each planting hole with a layer of leaf-mould. Mint: increase by root divisions; lift clumps, discard woody centres; replant shoots in semi-shade. Chives: flavouring in soups and salads in place of onions. Lift and divide into clumps of six bulbs. Replant clumps 6 in. apart. Mix wood ash with soil.

To prevent boxes of seedlings from failure through 'damping-off' the soil should be sterilised before seeds are sown, or the seedlings transferred to fresh pans or boxes when pricking-out. The trouble is caused by a minute fungus in the soil. To kill this, stir into a gallon of water a pinch of permanganate of potash; spray with this solution, or pour boiling water through the soil, or bake the soil in an oven for two hours.

Prepare compost for transplanting seedlings as shown. Make holes in this for the reception of the seedlings from 2 to 4 in. apart, according to size. Never touch the seedlings when pricking-out or they may be injured. Cut two match-sticks as above. Loosen soil with the pointed one held in the left hand, lift the plants out with the other. Press them in the compost, water with fine rose, and shade from sun for a few days then expose to light and air.

Plant out sweet peas on a warm day in soil already raked. Do not turn out more than a few at a time from boxes or pots, as the roots get dry. Use a trowel, making holes 6 in. deep. Pots of four to five plants may be planted undisturbed after turning them out, otherwise allow 6 in. between single plants. Get rid of plantains and dandelions by hand-weeding. Cuttings of border chrysanthemums in pots in a frame, when rooted, are potted separately as shown.

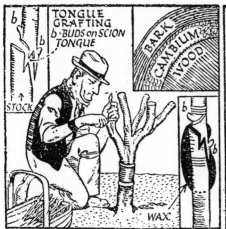

Grafting restores exhausted trees and produces fruit on parts of trees on which it was previously lacking. The scions or grafts must be ripe shoots of previous year's growth in an almost dormant state, while the sap in the stock, the tree or branch to which they are to be attached, must be running freely, and side branches removed. The scion must be fixed in the stock so that the cambium layers, the seat of growth just behind the bark, are in contact.

Tongue grafting is usually employed when the stock is young. The 6-in. long, one-year-old scion, having four buds, is cut through the wood between two buds growing on opposite sides, the sloping cut narrowing to a point just below the lowest bud. The tongue is cut to correspond with downward cut made in the stock, prepared as seen. Bind with raffia, leaving lowest bud free, then cover with grafting wax.

Crown grafting is done by cutting downward from top of branch stump where scions are to go, deep enough to penetrate bark. This is raised on either side. Prepared scions are slipped down between. Bind exposed cuts and cover. In saddle grafting the scion is cut with two tails which fit over stock. Cleft grafting is usually done when tree is old. Split branch end. Scions with shaped ends are slipped in cleft, held apart with a wedge. The wax is made with tallow one part, bees-wax two parts, and resin four parts, melted together, and used hot.

Shoots of last summer's growth on the mauve-flowered *Buddleia variabilis* are cut back to within 3 in. of the older wood; thin out all weak twigs. Late flowering kinds of *Ceanothus*, or Californian lilac, should have last summer's strong shoots cut by half; cut out all weak shoots. Reduce the number of new shoots on hardy hydrangeas to obtain good heads of bloom. Cut *Hypericum calycinum* (rose of Sharon or Aaron's beard) to within a few inches of the ground.

Choice evergreen shrubs can be planted now while the roots are active. Do not allow roots to become dry. Water before and after planting. Place a mulch of leafmould or decayed manure above the roots of newly planted shrubs. Now is a safe time to transplant conifers. Dig a 1 ft. deep trench around the tree, about 1½ ft. from it; cut off the tips of the roots. Having previously dug the fresh hole ready to receive it, replant at once, covering the roots layer by layer with welltrodden soil.

Before planting clematis mix mortar rubble with the soil. They are usually sold in pots, which makes the planting an easy matter. Choose a partly shaded position; a north or west wall is ideal, the best soil being chalky loam. Terminal shoots of aucuba inserted in sandy soil under glass, as shown, will form roots in a few weeks, to be then planted out, The aucuba is one of the best evergreens for planting beneath trees.

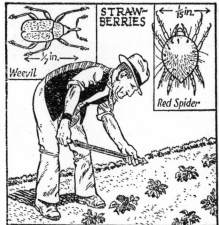

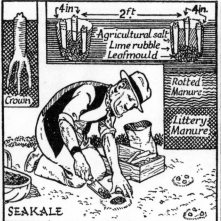

During this month and next the strawberry weevils emerge. Small round holes in the plant leaves denote their presence. The buds are next attacked; an egg is laid in a hole bitten in each bud. Derris, used as dust or a spray, is effective. A poisonous lead arsenate dust can also be used. Another foe of the plants is red spider. Spray the crowns now with lime sulphur, using 1 pint of concentrated solution to 4 gallons of water, or dust with flowers of sulphur.

Blanched seakale shoots are the favourite vegetable of some people. Easy to grow, it has the merit of being free from pests and disease. Two-year-old crowns are set singly, the bluish crown end being uppermost, in drained soil, prepared as shown. Work in top soil a bucketful of lime rubble per square yard and rake in the trodden surface 1 oz. per square yard of the salt. Rooted cuttings are set in groups of three 4 in. apart, the groups being 2 ft. apart.

Kohl-rabi, the turnip-rooted cabbage, has a 'nutty' flavour which appeals to many. The ball-shaped stem, used when it attains the size of a tennis ball, is the part eaten. Do not peel before cooking. It is sown successively now and until the end of July in rows 2 ft. apart. Sow thinly. Thin the seedlings to 6 in. apart. Use a dressing of freshly slaked lime as a safeguard against club-root.

Now is the time to make an asparagus bed. Choose a sunny site. The bed, 4 ft. wide, should run north and south. Dig the soil out 2 ft. deep. Prepare it similarly to the method in the inset. Badly drained soil is useless. If soil is heavy, fork sand or burnt earth into the top 8 in. Salt is most useful on very light sandy soil; superphosphate, 2 oz. per square yard, can also be forked into the surface.

Dig a trench 1 ft. wide, 9 in. deep, drawing the sides to the centre, thus making a ridge about 7 in. below soil level. Spread a fine layer of leaf-mould and sand along the ridge top. If you want a small crop the first year, choose three-year-old crowns. Two-year-old crowns will give you a crop the second year. One-year-old crowns will necessitate a wait of three years before cutting.

Having cut off all damaged roots, soak the crowns in water and plant them at once. Set them 15 in. apart, spreading the roots down each side of the ridge. Fill in the soil, firm it and take out the next trench in the same way. Rake the bed surface evenly, sloping it slightly from the centre to prevent water becoming stagnant. Make an alley around the bed, and finally give it a mulch of well-decayed manure 2 in. deep.

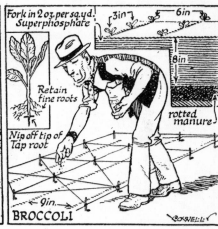

Celeriac, turnip-rooted celery, is easy to grow, needs no blanching; its flavour is similar to celery; it can be stored or left in the ground, and will keep for a long time after fully grown. Sow in boxes nearly filled with a compost as shown. Cover seed lightly, make soil firm and moisten with tepid water. Cover the boxes with glass and brown paper, place in warmth; wipe and turn glass daily and remove these coverings when seed has germinated.

Prick out seedlings 3 in. apart when quite small into other boxes filled with six parts soil, two parts sand and peat, adding small quantities of sulphate of potash, if procurable, superphosphate and lime. Harden off in a cold frame, and plant out in the open in May and June in deeply dug soil with decayed vegetable refuse buried 8 in. deep. Set the young knobs on and not below the surface, on light soil in shallow trenches and on a slightly raised bed if soil is heavy.

On a firm seed-bed on the south side of the garden sow broccoli in shallow drills 9 in. apart, stretching black thread across to protect seedlings from birds, and dust Brassisan powder as a preventive against club-root. Transplant seedlings to a firm bed, as shown. Cut off tip of tap root, but do not injure the finer roots. Later on plant out at 2 ft. apart each way. Hoe frequently between the seedlings to keep the weeds down.

Although usually made of galvanised wire, baskets suspended from the roof of a greenhouse can be made of other materials. One which is made from cement laid on a paper-covered flower-pot, the pot being removed when the cement has set, is seen in insets A, B and C. Three screweyes to carry the suspension chains are cemented at equal points. Thinned red umber and turps will improve its appearance.

The method of filling the baskets with a lining of live moss and suitable compost is shown. This is done by placing the basket on a large flower-pot. Insert the plants at the sides as well as the top. Arrange those of drooping growth around the sides, and dwarf plants of upright growth on top. Ivy-leafed and zonal geraniums, alyssum, verbena, *Phlox drummondii*, ageratum, *Cineraria maritima* and fuchsia are all suitable.

Hang the baskets in the greenhouse for a few weeks, gradually harden the plants off, and place out of doors during June. Hardy plants, such as those named in the inset, can be in baskets out of doors permanently. The best method of watering the baskets is by immersing them in a bath of water in which a pot is placed for standing each one on. It is very necessary to keep the soil moist in summer.

Ridge cucumbers attain a good size if grown at the foot of a sunny fence or wall. Dig ground deeply and manure it liberally. Sow two or three seeds together in groups, 2 ft. apart. If your soil is clay, dig circular holes 3 ft. across, 1 ft. deep; fill with partly decayed manure, then cover with 6 in. of soil. If sown or planted in rows, allow 4 ft. between rows. A good method is to make mounds 2 ft. apart. Each has two pailfuls of manure.

Cover each heap with an inch of fine soil and place on the top a 6-in. layer of a compost made of loam 4 parts, and 1 part each of old manure and sand, using 1 oz. bonemeal per pailful. Press compost and sow two seeds 2 in. apart, ½ in. deep, in the middle of each heap. Place the seeds on their sides to help germination. Water after sowing. Cover each pair with an inverted pot until seedlings appear.

Protect seedlings with brushwood in cold weather. If growing cucumbers in a frame, place a layer of fermenting manure along the bottom and build on this a bed 6 in. deep of compost made as shown. Place a mound of soil 6 in. high beneath each light. Set one plant on each mound. Syringe with sun-warmed water all over twice daily. To grow cucumbers successfully, a moist atmosphere must be maintained.

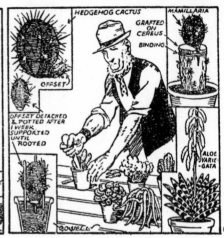

Succulent plants, such as cacti, of which there are many varieties, can be raised from seed sown in pots or pans of sandy compost placed on a thick layer of drainage crocks and pieces of broken brick. The seeds are just covered with fine soil, watered, and glass placed on the pots till germination takes place. When large enough, they are pricked out at 1 in. apart and later potted singly.

Some kinds of cacti, being of a drooping growth, are sometimes grafted on to others having erect stems. *Pereskia aculeata*'s stem, cut off at the top, with a wedge-shaped piece removed, makes a suitable stock into which pieces of rat's tail cactus or *Epiphyllum truncatum*, cut to shape, are slipped in and fixed with pins or cacti spines. Put grafted plants in glass-covered boxes in warmth till the union is formed.

Cactus plants can be increased by cuttings. Cut pieces from stems or any part of the plants, lay aside to form a corky skin over the cuts, then insert in pots of equal parts loam and sand. Do not water till roots form, which will be hastened by bottom heat. Propagating cacti by offsets is explained above. Keep established succulents moist in summer, dry in winter. They flower best when roots are cramped in small pots.

Whether you have raised your own tomato seedlings or are buying your plants, it is well to note the healthiest are those that are short-jointed and stocky, with dark green leaves. Lanky stems and pale foliage denote weakness. When the pots, which have been kept near the glass (A) are filled with roots, the plants are moved to larger ones. When established, harden them off gradually in a cold frame. If a bed of soil is prepared in a frame, tomatoes can be grown in it during the summer.

Dig two spits deep. In the lower half incorporate fibrous loam, three parts to one of rotten manure, adding crushed mortar rubble, bonemeal and sand. Give a top dressing of hydrated lime and a good sprinkling of wood ashes. Cultivation in large pots or boxes in a cold greenhouse is shown here. Plant firmly, water thoroughly when necessary. Never allow roots to get dry. Ventilate freely, but avoid risk of chilling and draughts.

On a bed, prepared as shown, at the foot of a sunny wall or fence, outdoor tomato plants should give good results. Water the plants the day previous to transplanting to open ground, and again after replanting, the best way being to sink flower pots against each plant and fill them when needed. Set plants 18 in. apart. Tie each stem to a 4 ft. stake. Remove all side shoots when large enough to pinch out.

Make a window-box of wood 1 in. thick, 9 in. deep at the back, the length of the sill, and slightly projecting over the front edge. To bring the top level, place wedges under the box and a tray to catch surplus water, or the sides and front can have a continuation bevelled to the proper angle. Fix the bottom of the box level so that it does not touch the sill; it should have drainage holes. Fix hooks on sides for attaching the box to walls or woodwork.

Cork bark, either nailed along the front or to a separate board made to hook over the front, gives a rustic effect. Paint the box and burn paper to char the inside till the wood is burned 1/8 in. deep; this prevents rot. Place a 2-in. layer of crocks or small stones on the bottom, cover this with reversed turf or leaves, and fill to within 1 in. of the top with a compost of light soil and sand.

Suitable plants for a shady window are *Begonia semperflorens* pansies, petunias, fuchsia, musk and creeping jenny, dwarf plants being arranged along the front. *Begonia lloydi*, in various colours, droops well, while for the climbers at the sides use nasturtium and canary creeper. Calceolarias, stocks, lobelias and geraniums are other suggestions. Don't forget that window-boxes can be made use of all the year round.

Bark-ringing checks excessive growth of fruit trees and helps to develop fruiting spurs. It should be done this month when sap is running freely. With the point of a sharp knife cut round the edges of a half-ring on the stem, a little below the lowest branches. Peel off the bark down to the hard white wood. Four inches below this cut another half-ring on the opposite side of the stem, beginning and ending immediately below the top one. They should be ½ in. deep.

Paint the cuts with lead paint. Another way is to cut a complete ring, not more than ¼ in. deep, right round the stem of the tree. The strip of bark must peel off cleanly. To prevent disease entering, the cut must heal over during the season. Cover it with grafting wax or a strip of adhesive tape. Bark-ringing is particularly useful on apple and pear trees. Stone fruit trees may be treated, but on these there is a risk of 'gumming.'

White woolly threads on apple trees are a sign of an attack of American blight or woolly aphis (see X). This pest sucks the sap, particularly on wounds or cracks in the bark and may allow canker fungi to obtain a hold, causing galls or swellings to form (see Y), leading to weakening of the tree. The 'wool' hides young aphides; both these and wingless females do damage. Brush affected parts with a stiff brush dipped in shellac, 1 oz., dissolved in one pint methylated spirit.

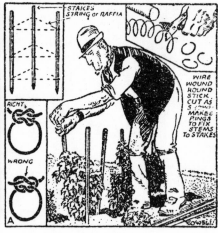

After tulips have finished flowering they may be left in the ground until the leaves have turned yellow, then lifted and stored. If the ground is needed, take up plants without damaging roots, and replant in a 3-in. deep trench on a shaded reserve border. When leaves have died, take up bulbs and store until needed for planting in autumn. If tulips are left undisturbed they may deteriorate after the first season.

Among half-hardy annuals raised under glass to be planted out now are: Nemesia; set 6 in. apart in exposed position in soil enriched with decayed manure. Cosmos, 18 in. to 3 ft. high, various colours, long stems making them useful for cutting; plant in well-drained soil. not rich, in sheltered sunny position. Kochia, a small bush with beautiful leaf-colouring. Salpiglossis; set about 1 ft. apart in sunny position.

Most plants need support to prevent damage from wind, etc. Stakes, preferably painted green, should be set in position before the stems are fully grown; two or three pieces of green raffia or string should be tied round the three stakes set to each plant. Inset (A) shows a good and a bad knot for tying to a stake. When a single plant stem is staked, as the tomato, it is best to tie the stem round first before tying to support.

Make further sowings of early kinds of carrots for autumn use, rotted manure being incorporated in the lower spit only; and old soot, potting soil and wood ash with top soil. Carry out first thinning to 2 in. directly seedlings are ready, later to 6 in. apart. Do this after sunset, when there is less chance of trouble from the carrot-fly. Effect of destruction is shown in (A). Mulches of lawn mowings and dustings of powdered naphthalene are preventive measures against this pest.

Reduce beetroot seedlings as soon as they can be handled, globe type to 4 in. apart and 6 in. in the case of long-rooted kinds. Dust sulphàte of ammonia or nitrate of soda between rows, 1 oz. per 12 ft., avoiding foliage. Beet-fly maggots feed on leaves. Pinch 'blisters' on the leaves to kill the pests, give a dressing of nitrate of soda, and roll lightly just before thinning to crush maggots: it will not harm the plants.

When lettuce plants are 1 in. long plant them out 6 in. apart for small kinds and 9 in. for the larger kinds. Thinnings can be replanted at same distances on another bed. Dust sulphate of ammonia along rows (1 oz. per 12 ft.), but not on foliage or after hearts are forming. Pinch out growing tips of broad beans when two or three clusters of pods have set. Plant out various kinds of brassicas as shown.

Use grass clippings from lawn as a mulch to conserve moisture around rose trees and fruit bushes. Expose soot to air for a few days and it will make a dressing for the lawn; the green of the turf will be restored after rain. Disbud some of the roses which produce too many buds. Where three buds appear at the end of a shoot, remove the side ones, allowing the third to develop fully.

It is not too late to sow another row of peas. Those appearing must be protected from damage by birds. A framework placed at each end of the row with black threads stretched between will suffice. Peas should be supported early with twiggy sticks to which the tendrils will cling. Set the supporting sticks leaning slightly outwards, and not with their tops meeting over the centre of the rows.

Plants should be watered thoroughly the day before being potted or repotted. Water should run through the soil quickly in a correctly potted plant. Water pot-plants only when they need it, and then do it thoroughly. If, when lifted, a pot-plant feels heavy, no water is needed (inset A). If a ringing sound is heard on tapping it the soil is dry (B). Keep the top soil in pots stirred occasionally

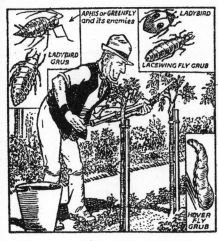

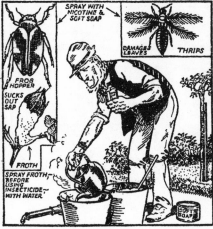

Among pests which attack rose trees the aphis or green-fly is the most common. They weaken the shoots by sucking the sap and cause fungous disease. Natural checks are ladybirds and their grubs, hover-flies, lacewing-flies and others; avoid destroying these useful insects. When using contact insecticides, the pests themselves must be well covered with the liquid.

Many effective remedies can be made up easily. Paraffin emulsion is made by dissolving a handful of soft soap in hot water, adding an eggcupful of paraffin while hot, after removing from fire. Stir well and add water to make up two gallons. While using, stir to prevent paraffin from floating. To every ten gallons of water add ¾ oz. of nicotine and some soft soap: this makes a good spray.

Derris powder is made up as a spray similarly, but this and nicotine may also be applied as a dust by means of small bellows. Choose a calm, wind-less day when using powders, spraying lightly with water previously to make the powder adhere. The advantage of using derris lies in the fact that, besides being a contact insecticide, it is also a stomach poison, particularly effective in the control of aphids.

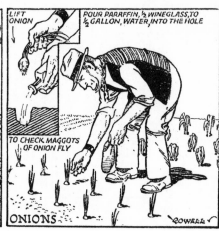

Maize or indian corn is a nourishing vegetable and decorative in growth. Prepare the soil as shown, and set seeds or seedlings in a warm, sunny position. Never allow plants to become dry. Mulch them with lawn mowings. Choose an early variety. To find out whether the corn is ready for gathering strip back the covering sheath, remove the silklike 'brush' and press the cob with your finger-nail; if a milky substance appears the cob is ripe enough for use. Quickly grown maize takes less time to cook than that of slow growth.

If you plant out your brussels sprouts seedlings on a site already well manured for a previous crop there will be no need to dig it deeply again; otherwise, prepare it as shown. If the variety chosen is of the tall growing kind, allow more space between plants than that shown. If you do not plant out in showery weather water the seedlings in. Dust soil with a club-root preventive preparation. Utilise space between rows by sowing lettuce, radish or spinach. Dust plants with derris powder to destroy green-fly, caterpillars and flea beetle.

When hoeing onions do not allow soil to mount up against the bulbs; draw it away so that they are exposed. Do not water unless quite necessary, and then do so to reach roots thoroughly. If foliage of any plants turn yellow, lift them out and pour paraffin and water in the holes to destroy maggots of onion-fly, and water the rows with it, keeping the mixture well stirred. Spread old soot and salt on the bed in showery weather. If mould forms on leaf tips mildew is indicated. Dust early morning with one part quick-lime and two parts flowers of sulphur.

If successive sowings of the fairy primrose are made, plants will bloom nearly all the year. Sown now, plants bloom in autumn. Sow calceolaria now in the same compost as shown. The seed being small, it is best to mix it with sand, a sprinkling of which is all that is needed for covering. Moisten soil three hours before sowing. Paper and glass coverings are removed from pans as soon as seed germinates.

Vines under glass should have the tips of all laterals nipped off at the second leaf beyond the bunch of berries. These bunches should be thinned when berries attain the size of small peas. Use long-pointed scissors, and a forked stick to steady the bunch. Do not touch the berries with hands. Cut out those which are discoloured, leaving all berries about ½ in. apart. Pot chrysanthemums finally, stake securely, and sink in bed of ashes in shade.

The axle of the rotating cutters in back drum mowers is raised or lowered by screws; the cutters should scrape the knife or bottom blade equally. In side wheel mowers the knife is movable; by slackening or tightening pairs of screws the edge is brought closer to, or farther from, the cylinder blades. By raising the rollers the front of the machine is tilted down, and so the knife is brought nearer the ground, thus cutting the grass shorter than if the rollers were lowered. To clean the knife, turn the machine on its side and use an old toothbrush.

Prepare a bed for mushrooms out of doors or in a dark, dry shed or cellar. The beds are composed mainly of fresh strawy manure, which should be stacked under cover to protect it from rain. Turn it over every few days for a fortnight to release gases and reduce heat. The best position for an outdoor bed is under trees or against a north wall. The temperature of the heap should be about 75 degrees. To test this, thrust a stick into the centre; if, when withdrawn, it is not too hot to hold, the temperature is right.

Before making the bed, fork the site to a depth of 1 ft. and place a layer of cinders over it. The bed should be about 2 ft. 6 in. wide at the base, ridged to a flat width of 1 ft. at the top. Build up in layers of about 4 in., firming each as you proceed. The spawn, broken into small pieces about walnut size, is pressed 1 in. deep into the manure bed at 9 in. apart. Two days later dust the bed with pyrethrum powder against woodlice.

Four days after spawning cover the bed with a layer of moist sifted soil and granulated peat. A week later cover the soil with a 6-in. layer of clean straw. When making a bed in a dark cellar or light-proof shed the bed is best made up in a wooden frame, as shown. Similar coverings to outdoor beds are made. If after about a month the soil appears to be dry, it may be watered through a rose, using tepid water.

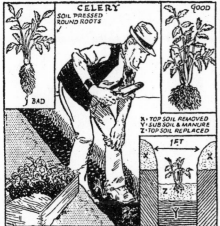

Celery plants grown in boxes can now be put out 9 in. apart in a 1-ft. wide trench, 10 in. deep. Place a layer of decayed manure in the trench about 4 in. deep. Tread the plants well in as each is planted. When all are planted, water them thoroughly. Later apply a dressing of nitrate of soda once a fortnight.

Dahlias in pots can be planted out in deeply dug soil in which decayed manure has been mixed. Water the dahlias the evening before planting. Allow 3 ft. between each – the more vigorous growers being 4 ft. apart. Use a trowel to make a hole large enough to take the full ball of unbroken soil. Stake soon after planting.

Use lawn sand on lawns infested with daisies and plantains; the method of making this is shown. The sand will turn the grass brown, but this will recover after about a week. When not too numerous, an old hand-fork will be useful in removing the weeds. A home-made weed extractor is shown in insets.

Unlike most flowering shrubs which benefit by pruning after flowering, rhododendrons and azaleas should be allowed to grow freely, but faded flower heads must be removed before seed can form. If the seed pods are not taken off, the shrub will lack vitality next season. When greenhouse azaleas have finished blooming, loosen soil before repotting (inset 1).

Marrows can still be planted out of doors after being hardened off. Plant on heap of decayed manure, garden refuse, or on a trellis. Moisture is essential; a depression round each stem will help water to percolate to the roots. When leading shoots are 2 ft. long, pinch out tops. When fruits have set, give liquid manure. If a poor crop is likely, carry out fertilisation as in inset.

Keep roots of sweet peas moist or the buds will fall before the blooms open. Restrict plants to one or two stems and remove all side shoots. Rub out these laterals with finger and thumb. The tendrils need not be cut off. Keep soil surface stirred with hoe. During flowering period, give soot water or liquid manure: one part diluted with four parts water.

To propagate hydrangeas choose the ends of non-flowering shoots having two or three pairs of leaves; remove the lowest pair, and make a cut just below a joint. Insert cuttings, either singly in 2½-in. pots, or three round the edge of 3½-in. pots, filled with sandy soil, putting silver sand in each hole. Water and put in closed cold frame under a handlight out of doors. Shade from sunlight, and syringe with tepid water.

Other cuttings which may be taken now are pansies and violas. Choose sturdy shoots which have no flower ends, those which spring from the base being best. Remove the lower leaves, cut below a joint, leaving a 'heel.' Strike the cuttings in boxes or pots of sandy soil placed in a frame where they will develop into strong plants. Named varieties of violas must be increased by cuttings.

Apart from its use as a weed remover, the Dutch hoe should be used throughout the garden where possible to assist plants in dry weather by breaking up the surface soil. Before feeding plants or trees with liquid manure, water them well – the fertiliser will then reach the roots. Cut off all dead blooms, old stems and seed pods. If this is done, in many cases they will flower again.

55

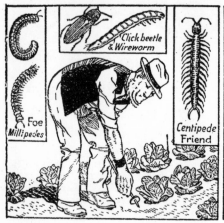

Wireworms are among the most harmful soil pests. They are the larvæ of the click beetle, ¼ in. to ½ in. long, thin, with a hard, deep, yellow, glossy skin, having three pairs of legs near the head. Do not confuse them with centipedes, which are similar in colour, flatter and have many legs along the length of the body. They do not damage plants, but feed on injurious insects. These again may be mistaken for millipedes, rooteating pests which coil up when disturbed. Traps to catch soil pests can be set by putting slices of potato or carrot speared with sticks just below the soil surface. Examine them daily.

Temporary curling of the top leaves of tomato plants may be due to too low a night temperature or draught. If leaf curling continues it may be due to manure or fertiliser burning the roots through not being mixed with the soil properly. Tap the pots to test their need of water; if a hollow sound is produced give the roots a soaking then withhold water until needed again. If the tops of plants continue to droop the cause may be sour soil or root decay. Scoop some soil from roots and water with lime water, add more good soil mixed with a little lime, heaping it around the stem (see A).

Keep constant watch for aphis or green-fly on fruit trees. If destroyed at their early stage a lot of worry will be saved later. Spray the leaves well with one of the well-known brands of dusting powders. Give another application ten days later. This will also be effective against pests which eat the leaves and those which curl within them. One way of dealing with the ant nuisance is to place inverted pots over the nests. Water around rims each day. After a few days part of the nest will have been transferred to the pots. Slip card under pot and drop contents into salted water (inset B).

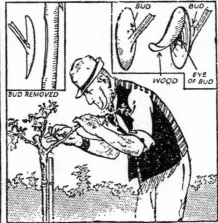

Choose showery weather if possible for rose-budding during this or next month, when the sap is running freely. The buds to take from the parent tree must be plump and healthy lower ones on a long shoot. Cut off the leaves. Insert a sharp knife about an inch above the eye, making a semicircular cut, slicing the bud from stem. Turn it over and with the thumb-nail prise up the wood under the bark and pull it sharply, peeling it out of the shell.

If there is a hole under the seat of the bud or the wood contains a projection, the bud is spoilt and a fresh one must be taken. A longitudinal incision is made in the bark of the stock to receive the bud, near the base of the branch on a standard or close to the ground on a dwarf. At the top of the cut make another horizontally, thus forming a T. Carry out the work quickly, so that neither the cut stock nor prepared bud can dry out.

Raise the bark on each side and insert the lower end of the bud shield, pushing it down. Cut upper end if it projects beyond the cross-cut and secure it firmly with bast or wool, leaving the bud exposed. Loosen the tie in three weeks if the joint has swollen, for in that case the union will have been achieved. If the weather is very dry, keep the stocks watered. No growth can generally be expected from the buds until the following spring.

A gardening problem which arises just now is how to keep the soil sufficiently moist to satisfy plants' needs and at the same time keep within the essential limits of water usage. In a dry, cracked soil the moisture is allowed to evaporate and so is lost. Mere surface watering is useless. By covering the soil or mulching it with materials, such as peat moss, coconut fibre, decayed garden refuse and lawn mowings, the moisture is retained and at the same time plant food is provided.

But it is useless to apply a mulch to a dry soil; this will only encourage the roots to strike upwards. Water and loosen the soil first. The mulch should not be placed right up against the plant stem. Place it in a 3-in. thick hollowed ring around each plant, or alongside, but a few inches away from rows of plants, as in (A). Inset (B) shows how to mulch a standard tree. If the mulching material offends the eye, cover it with fine dry soil. Keep the hoe going between all crops, too.

Slugs, which in some seasons cause so much damage to plants, favour damp conditions and feed mainly at night. To keep these pests away sprinkle lime, soot or powdered coke around seedlings, etc., frequently renewing the substance used in wet weather. If applied heavily, lime or dry Bordeaux powder will kill them. Drop any slugs found into salt and water. The methylated spirit, or meta tablet, and bran method will both attract and kill if spread around plants or on a tile. Naphthalene mixed with the garden rubbish heap will also kill slugs.

58

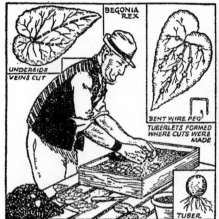

Many greenhouse plants with fleshy leaves can be easily propagated by means of leaf cuttings. Fully grown, well-developed leaves should be chosen; young or old hard ones are unsuitable. Cut through or notch the main veins or ribs on the under surface where they join. Lay the leaves in pans or boxes filled with a compost of loam, leaf-mould and sand, the notched or cut side in close contact with the soil, using U-shaped wire pegs for this purpose.

Set the pans in a glass-covered box in the greenhouse, keeping soil moist and shaded. In warm, moist conditions, small plants will develop at the cuts, which, when rooted, are taken off and potted singly. *Begonia rex* and *Gloire de Lorraine*, gloxinia, streptocarpus and echeverias can be treated in this way. *Begonia rex* leaves can also be cut and inserted upright, as shown. In the case of saintpaulia the whole leaf with stalk is used, tiny tubers forming at the ends.

Roots of anchusa, bouvardia, Oriental poppy, iris, clematis, pæony, Japanese anemone and *Romneya coulteri* can be cut into pieces set upright or horizontally in boxes or pans of sandy soil with little soil covering. The boxes are put in a cold frame until rooted, when they are planted out on a reserve border. When in the frame, place the pans on upturned flower pots as a safeguard against soil-pest attacks, when the young shoots show.

When layering carnations choose strong shoots, making a slicing cut in each just below and towards a joint, but do not sever the shoot. This cut must be held open when layered so that a root is formed. A small pebble will do. Peg down the layer with a wooden peg or hairpin into a little heap of loam, leaf-mould and coarse sand.

Pinks are propagated by pipings. These are the tops of shoots pulled out and so separated at a joint. They are planted 4 in. apart out of doors in a sandy compost in a shady position. Handlights should be placed over them. They may also be layered. When the layers are rooted, sever and transplant in sand in a shallow drill.

Similarly, strawberries are layered, choosing the best runners, and using the first plantlet only on each runner, cutting off beyond this. The plantlets are pegged down close to the joint or node. They may be layered into pots of sand to facilitate moving when rooted. When the runner plant is well rooted, sever the running stalk; this will be about three weeks after layering.

Tomatoes, like most other crops, are liable to various diseases, but with careful management most troubles can be avoided or overcome. In wet seasons one of the commonest affecting outdoor tomatoes is blight. If infected potatoes are growing nearby they will in turn infect the tomatoes. The leaves develop purple spots and a white mould at the edges; the fruits have brown spots. Remove affected leaves, etc., and spray weekly with Bordeaux mixture.

Stripe or streak does not attack outdoor tomatoes. The stems become marked with dark brown streaks, causing brittleness. The leaves may have yellow-green patches and turn inwards, and sometimes the fruits have pale brown sunken spots. Restore the plants to healthy condition by using sulphate of potash at the rate of 2 oz. per square yard once fortnightly. Plants allowed to become dry at roots and then given water too generously cause fruits to split (inset X).

Mildew or leaf-mould does not often attack outdoor tomatoes. Damp, humid conditions in the greenhouse favour the disease, which is recognisable by the mould causing pale yellow patches on upper leaf surfaces, the under parts then becoming grey. Do not allow temperature to get too high. Always water in the morning and give ample ventilation. Spray or dust with sulphur. Remember a damp greenhouse will help the disease to grow.

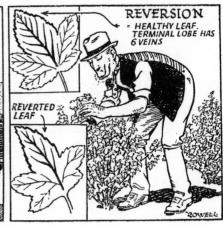

Soon after the berries are gathered from summer-fruiting raspberries all old canes which have fruited should be cut down near to ground level and burned, leaving only strong canes of this year's growth. By carrying out the summer pruning at this period pests and diseases in the old canes are destroyed and the remaining young canes are able to grow freely. Cut out and burn all unhealthy, weak and crowded growths, leaving four to six canes only to each clump. These should be spaced out when tying loosely to the supports.

Look to the leaves of your celery plants. If any have 'blisters' formed on them it is a sign of trouble from celery-fly maggots. Spray with ¼ oz. of nicotine and ¼ lb. soft soap to 2½ gallons water. Bend back outer leaves in search of slugs; place any found in salt water. Pinch off all side shoots and cut off any outer leaves turning yellow. If your plants have spread out too much in early stages tie stems together loosely just below the leaves. Keep soil at bottom of trench loosened with a hand fork.

If black currant bushes provide few or no berries, yet have produced plenty of bloom, they may be suffering from reversion or nettle-leaf. Often only one branch is affected at first. Trouble may be detected by counting the veins on the lower surface of leaves. A normal leaf has five to seven veins in the terminal lobe; if it has less than five reversion is present. Affected leaves are usually smaller and more pointed than healthy ones. Badly affected bushes should be burned. Remove suspected fruitless branches.

Before leaving for holiday it is well to take a few precautions. Ferns, palms, and other pot-plants, if well rooted, can be put in a large bath in which the water reaches half-way up the pots. Place the bath in a shady spot. Keep the soil in pot-plants damp by connecting strips of flannel from each with a bucket of water. Room plants will be better outside, where they will be exposed to any rainfall.

Clip all hedges and evergreen shrubs and trees. Cut off all dead or dying flowers and untidy shoots from bedding plants. Mow the lawn thoroughly; hoe the soil well in beds and borders, and see that all supporting stakes are firm. The soil around wall fruit trees should be mulched with decayed manure. This will keep it moist and benefit the fruits.

Pot-plants can also be plunged to their rims in soil or ashes, covering the surface soil with fibre or leafmould, and watering well. Other methods are: damp moss placed on soil or pot-plants; pots stood in saucers of water, or raised from the staging, and a length of lamp-wick or cotton wool inserted through drainage hole, the other end being in a bowl of water.

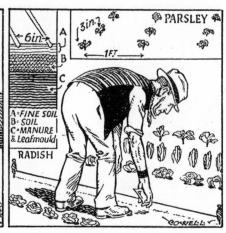

When shallot stalks have turned yellow no further growth develops. Scrape soil from around the bulbs and bend tops over to assist ripening. When this has taken place ease them out of the ground with a fork, preferably on a sunny day. Dry well for two days by hanging them in the sun. If weather prevents open-air drying spread them on a shelf in a dry, airy shed. When quite dry break up the clusters and store them in wide-meshed baskets or net bags so that air circulates around them.

Having prepared the site in spring for final planting out of leeks set them 10 in. apart in rows 18 in. apart, preferably in showery weather, or water the soil well previously. Lift each plant with a ball of soil. Shorten longest leaves to help root growth. Plant either in trenches or on the flat. Use a dibber to make a hole for each; drop plant in without filling hole with soil. Rain will do that gradually and so blanch when full growth is attained. If planted in trenches put brown paper tubes, round the plants, kept in position by small stakes and a little soil drawn up at the base. As growth proceeds lift the tube higher and earth up more soil at the base.

Main sowing of spring cabbages is made during the next few weeks. Avoid sappy growth by not sowing on rich soil. Sow very thinly in drills 6 in. apart. Stretched black thread or evergreen branches will protect seedlings. Transplant to nursery bed when fourth leaf forms, putting them 4 in. apart in rows 6 in. apart. Other sowings to make now include radishes in drills on rich bed of fine soil free from stones, in a cool, damp spot. Parsley is sown thinly on well worked soil in drills 1 ft. apart. Thin to 3 in. apart, later to 1 ft. apart. Month-old soot water promotes growth.

ESCH—SCHOLTZIA · CORNFLOWER · NIGELLA · LARKSPUR · SCABIOUS

SOW IN NARROW DRILLS. RAKE LIGHTLY AFTER

CARD TO KEEP RAMBLER ROSE CUTTING BELOW WATER IN JAR.

YEW or TAXUS CUTTING SET IN SANDY SOIL IN A COLD FRAME.

By choosing a vacant space in the vegetable garden, near the edge for preference, in which to sow some of the hardy annuals now instead of waiting to sow them in spring, where they are to flower, their period of development will be lengthened. They can easily be transplanted in spring, and, though a few may suffer in winter, many will survive to become finer plants than those sown in spring. To those shown here, the Shirley poppy may be added.

The pruning of rambler roses should be done soon after the blooms have faded. It is worth while detaching all shoots from their supports, laying them on the ground, and cutting out all old wood which will be replaced by the new vigorous shoots developing later; these will mature by being fully exposed to sun and air. Some shoots can be used as cuttings to form roots in jars of water in the way shown.

Evergreen hedges, such as yew and holly, can be clipped this month. A taut line stretched along the top of a hedge will be found an aid to neatness and accuracy when clipping. Short shoots with a heel may be used as cuttings, by removing the lower leaves and inserting the shoots in sandy soil in a cold frame ventilated daily. This should be for a short time only, the frame being kept closed for a few weeks until the cuttings are rooted.

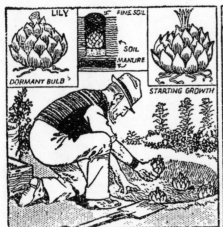

Plant madonna lilies during the next few weeks. They only root from the base; cover with 1 in. or 2 in. of soil. If the stems are vigorous and flower freely, do not transplant this lily. On coarse sand set the bulbs sloping so that moisture cannot collect in the scales. Plant belladonna lilies 5 in. deep, 1 ft. apart in soil excavated 2 ft., replaced with old turf, leaf-mould and decayed manure on a layer of broken bricks.

Plant 6 in. apart, 2 in. deep, colchicum in rock garden or in partial shade among leaf-losing trees. Small kinds can be potted in loam and leaf-mould and put in a cold greenhouse. Turn out old corms of Persian cyclamen and repot in fresh soil. Plant hardy cyclamens in shade in rock garden or on a border facing west or north-west. Add leaf-mould and rubble to the soil. Plant them 6 in. apart and 3 in. deep in a clump.

Among the early flowering bulbs which may be planted now are crocus, squill, winter aconite, chionodoxa or glory of the snow, and snowdrops. An indicator showing the depths in inches at which to plant various kinds of bulbs is seen in the inset. Sprinkle some sand in the holes. Basic slag, 8 oz. per square yard, and a little decayed manure as a top dressing, will enrich the soil.

We can help to avoid waste by making as much use as possible of everything in the garden. After the last gathering of broad beans crop, cut down the stems to within a few inches of the ground, fork the surface around them and water thoroughly. A fresh crop of new shoots will shortly be seen producing a second crop of pods of small beans which should be gathered regularly. When pulling radishes don't throw away the tops; they will provide a useful cooked vegetable.

Avoid wasting ground space by cutting off pea haulms close to ground level, after the crop has been gathered, leaving the roots in the soil. Fork the plot well, give it a dressing of superphosphate, 2 oz., and sulphate of potash, 1 oz., per square yard, then rake level, making ready for a sowing of an early variety of carrot and globe beet for use in autumn. Finely shredded young beet leaves are a good addition to salads and can be cooked like spinach.

Young nasturtium leaves and flowers and petals of pot marigold can also be used in salads; the latter are also useful for flavouring soups, stews, etc. Don't throw away rhubarb leaves. The water in which a few have been boiled is effective as a spray against aphides. It is wasteful to let perpetual spinach leaves grow large; they will be too coarse. Keep them constantly cut when young; use them for cooking or as a substitute for lettuce.

The most common fungoid pest likely to attack rose trees just now is mildew, appearing as white patches on leaves and tips of shoots. Unless checked this will cause them to crumple and fall, and may spread to the buds, producing 'suffocation.' Various remedies are shown here; perhaps the best is sulphur. Do not expose liver of sulphur to air until placed in water for spraying. Sulphur dust is effective, and can be bought, dyed green, to render it unnoticeable on leaves.

Where thin and bare patches appear on the lawn, renovate with an application of liquid nitrate of soda sprinkled over the surface. By crushing the nitrate of soda to a powder and using it as a top dressing it will serve as well in wet weather. An alternative stimulant, used in a similar way, is common salt. By loosening the soil where bare patches occur on the lawn, small tufts of grass, taken up when weeding beds, may be used; dibble them in a few inches apart.

Chrysanthemums should be fed every ten days. Give alternate doses of soot water and dried blood (one teaspoonful in a gallon of water). A special fertiliser may replace dried blood if desired. Remove buds below the terminal bud and the small shoots below the crown bud to stimulate growth as in inset (A). The pots should be stood on a bed of cinders. Plants are put under glass at the end of next month.

As a general rule apples should be just ripe when needed for dessert or storing; those not fully matured deteriorate in store. To ascertain whether the fruit is ready for gathering, raise it as shown in (A); if it comes off with a slight twist, picking may be started. Handle apples and pears carefully to prevent bruising; they keep better if wrapped separately in tissue or oiled paper, as in (B) and (C). A warm, close, dry store tends to cause apples to shrivel. The store-room must be dark, frost-proof and of even temperature.

Tiers of trays, such as in (D), make ideal storage places for late-keeping apples or stewing pears. A small quantity of pears may be suspended to beams, as in (E), in a cool, airy place. Another way to store sound apples is by placing a layer of straw in a box, packing the wrapped fruit in layers, sinking the box in the soil and covering with layers of straw and soil. Late-keeping culinary apples may also be stored out of doors in clamps, similar to those made for potatoes.

Plums and gages of dessert kinds, if picked when skins are dry, a day or so before quite ripening, may be stored for a week or two after gathering if dried and laid in shallow boxes in a cool, dark room. Stone fruits can be bottled as shown. When putting jars in oven don't put rubber rings on. Cooking takes rather less than 1 hour. When removing jars don't stand them on a cold surface. Pour boiling water in carefully to avoid cracking jars. Tighten screwband when cool; next day, test by lifting glass lid, which should be fast or sealing is not perfect. Replace and store in cool place.

Chionodoxa, or glory of the snow, hardy early flowering bulbs, growing about 8 in. high, thrive in ordinary soil. Plant them 2 to 3 in. deep, 3 in. apart in groups in rockery or borders. Kept in a cold frame, 6-in. pots of ten-twelve bulbs set in sandy loam, will flower well. Take them into the greenhouse when growth is visible. Colchicum are also suitable for rockery, among low-growing plants, in grass, or as pot-plants.

Eranthis, (winter aconite) yellow flowers, 4 in. high, one of the earliest to bloom, can be planted now in masses 2 in. deep. Narcissus and daffodil bulbs of two or three years' growth will usually have small bulbs, offsets, attached to the parent bulb. Take these off, plant on a spare border; they will bloom within one or two seasons. Before planting out of doors, scatter bonemeal 2 oz. per square yard on the soil and fork in; never use fresh manure.

Strawberry runners layered a few weeks ago should now be rooted. Cut the connecting stalk (inset A), dig up the plants and transfer them to the new bed. Manure should be worked in the top soil; scatter basic slag over the bed, 2 lb. per square yard. Set plants 18 in. apart in rows 2 ft. apart. Plant with trowel, not a dibber. Pinch out any runners that form during the first year.

Bend onion leaves over at the 'neck' to check further growth and encourage the ripening of the bulbs. When ready, lift onions with fork, taking care to avoid injuring them. Bulbs having thick, soft 'necks' do not keep very well (see A) and should be singled out and used before others. Leave bulbs on the bed if fine, or put them in greenhouse, frame or shed to dry before storing. Very warm conditions cause them to shrivel. Look them over and remove any showing signs of rot. Lift and store shallots as in (B).

Feed leeks with weak liquid manure or sprinkle a mixture along each side of the rows made of superphosphate of lime 5 parts, sulphate of ammonia 3 parts, using 2 oz. per yard run. Thin out carrots for autumn use at 3 in. apart (see C). Keep side shoots on tomato plants nipped out and feed with fertiliser alternately with weak liquid manure. Tie back leaves shading fruit (see D). Spray with Bordeaux mixture against blight, but not in sunlight.

To secure long white stems on celery start earthing up with trowel when plants are fully grown; not too firmly or hearts will be unable to expand. Remove offshoots round base. Before first earthing up drench trenches well. Earth up again a fortnight later as far as lower leaves with a spade, taking care not to let soil fall into hearts. Final earthing up is done later; this time only tips of leaves are left exposed.

Wingless female winter moths, woolly aphis, capsid bugs and other pests emerge from the ground, crawl up fruit tree stems in October and winter to deposit eggs on branches. The caterpillars hatch in spring and feed on foliage and fruit. To check these pests, a barrier is formed of paper bands, covered with special 'tacky' grease, which are fixed around the stems 1 ft. below the lower branches. If the bark is rough scrape it smooth first.

The bands are tied on tightly top and bottom. On uneven trunks fix drawing-pins in the hollows to prevent pests from crawling under the paper. Banding grease made for the purpose should be used, or prepared paper smeared with grease can be bought. Paint stem with limewash above the band. Keep bands free of dead leaves and the grease tacky by scraping it occasionally. Supporting stakes must also be grease-banded. Low radiating branches must each be banded.

Prepare soil for winter spinach, digging well and incorporating some decayed manure or a mixture of equal parts of fish manure and bonemeal. Prickly seeded or winter spinach is raised by sowing at two or three fortnightly intervals in shallow drills 9 in. apart. Thin seedlings to 6 in. apart. Choose a sheltered position. In severe weather give seedlings protection by means of cloches or glass-covered boxes.

Lift the main carrot crop before cold weather sets in. Cut off the leaves and store in dry soil or sand in a shed, or arrange in layers of ashes or sand in covered boxes. Place them so that the crowns are away from each other. If lack of space prevents storing in a shed make small clamps in a dry spot in the way shown. Do not store any damaged roots, and see that all are quite dry. The soil covering should be 3 in. thick.

If you cannot use all your vegetable marrows within a reasonable time you can store them. Choose only sound, ripe, green-streaked varieties. Hang them up in a dry place in cradles made of pairs of broad tape or cloth, suspended by hooks and sticks as shown. In this way they should keep in good condition until January or February. Take care not to bruise the skins. The temperature should not be allowed to fall below 45 degrees F.

Store parsnips in layers against a wall or fence as shown. Lift and dry onions thoroughly before storing in a dry, cool place, by hanging them in nets. Lift celeriac when the bulbous stems are blanched. Remove leaves and store them in sand in a dry, cool shed. In the south it may not be necessary to lift them. By drawing up the soil around the bulbs and covering the plants with straw or bracken they should be sufficiently protected.

This is the best period of the year in which to sow grass seed. The site for a new lawn must be dug 1 ft., all weeds removed and the soil forked several times. Drive pegs in to one level, testing this by laying a straight-edged board across the pegs with a spirit-level held on it. All soil must be smoothed down. Prick with fork the top soil before sowing.

The soil should be rolled, raked and rolled again before marking the site into equal sections with string and sticks. If each pound of seed is mixed with ¼ pint of cool quassia chips solution there will be no bird-robbing trouble. Boil 1 oz. quassia chips in two quarts of water for two hours. After sowing, the lawn must be rolled from end to end, and from side to side.

Cut out dead turfing in squares, break up the under soil with handfork, and loosen soil at underside of the new turf. Lay new turf in position and beat down with spade. Bare patches may be resown now in showery weather. Prick over top 2 in. and beat down with back of spade before sowing. Sift ¼-in. layer of soil over and roll. Sprinkle lawn mowings over repaired patches if weather is dry.

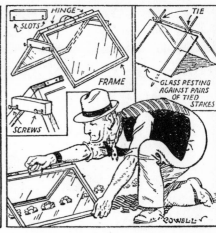

For a continuous supply of vegetables and salads during autumn and winter, glass-covering is very useful. The larger or 'barn' type of cloche, consisting of four panes of glass with wire supports, is used for crops of higher growth than those plants suitable for the 'tent' type, with two panes of glass. It is unnecessary to remove cloches for watering; the ground is watered close to outside of glass. Lettuce seed of kinds resistant to cold is sown in rows 1½ ft. apart under continuous cloches. They will then stand severe weather.

Another use for cloches is the prolongation of the supply of parsley. Trim off all old, coarse leaves, then cover with glass. Some roots can be lifted and packed with soil in a frame; the same can be done with mint. The wire supports can be dispensed with by using blocks of wood 1 in. thick, having pairs of slots cut at 45 degrees to hold the glass, as shown here.

Two frames – old picture frames will serve the purpose – hinged and held in place by a slotted block of wood at each end slipped over screws will make serviceable clothes. Odd pieces of glass resting against pairs of stakes tied together will also be useful to protect vegetable and salad crops and hasten the germination of seeds for early crops. Insert the ends of stakes into the soil.

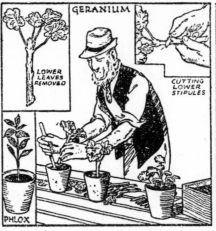

Root cuttings of anchusa can be taken now. The roots are exposed, sections cut off, divided into 2½-in. lengths, and placed end upwards in deep boxes of soil, the part nearest the stem being at the top. Cut the top end flat and the lower end slanting. Each piece should have a bud. They should be almost level with the surface of the soil 2 in. apart. When the roots and leaves have developed, pot them in 3-in. pots and put in the cold frame for the winter.

While still in the flower-bed firm side shoots of geraniums are cut off, the lower leaves and stipules removed, and the stem trimmed back to the lowest joint. They may be set singly in small pots, several in layer pots, or in boxes. Sand is sprinkled on the surface. Do not plant too deeply or too high. Do not water the soil until it appears quite dry. Proceed in this way until growth becomes active, then pot up separately.

Cut shoots of rambler, bush or climbing roses to a length to allow for trimming. When the lower leaves are removed and a cross-wise cut is made in the bottom they should be from 9 in. to 1 ft. long. Place them in a narrow trench lined with sifted leaf-mould and press the soil back against them. Non-flowering shoots of violas and pansies, trimmed and dipped in a soft-soap solution, are planted in a cold frame. Phlox cuttings are rooted in pots in a greenhouse.

Sow Lettuce and Radish between Asparagus beds

Unripe tomatoes can be wrapped separately. Keep in dark airy place.

use green tomatoes for chutney and pickles

Cut open. squeeze pulp, wash and strain two days later

Separate seeds & dry them on glass

Clear asparagus beds now the leaves have turned yellow, cutting down stems to within a few inches of ground. Remove weeds and pick up all fallen berries, as these contain seeds; self-sown seedlings are not wanted. If soil is light, top-dress bed, after clearing, with decayed strawy manure, to a depth of 2 in. covering it with a sprinkling of soil. On clay soil, defer manuring until March. Basic slag, 4 oz. per square yard, raked in, is beneficial. Paths between beds can be used for growing winter lettuce and radish.

Remove any large leaves shading tomatoes which are likely to ripen naturally; in most districts there is little chance of them doing so without aid after another week or so. Put any turning colour in a sunny window, turning them occasionally. They may be put, preferably wrapped singly in paper, in closed, but not airtight, boxes or drawers. The plants may be lifted carefully, hung roots uppermost, in a cool, dry place. Green tomatoes can be pickled or used to make chutney.

By choosing fully ripened tomatoes you may save the seeds for sowing next season. Cut them in halves, squeeze the pulp and seeds into an earthenware bowl. After two days wash and strain through a sieve, clearing the pulp away. Spread the seeds out on a sheet of glass. When quite dry store the seeds in paper bags. A dry cupboard is the best storage place. Although tomato seeds retain their vitality over a number of years, it is preferable to sow them as soon as possible.

Maincrop potatoes can be stored in either a mound or oblong-shaped clamp. Dig out a shallow trench around each site, which should be in an unexposed place, using the excavated soil as a base. Place over this a layer of ashes or straw. Heap the tubers on this in a cone or ridge shape. Cover heap with 4 in. of straw. When frosts begin, cover again with 6 in. of firmed soil. Insert tufts of straw into the top to give ventilation.

If several cauliflowers are ready for use at the same time, lift some with soil on roots. Hang them heads downwards in a cool, dark place; there they will keep in condition for a week or so (A). Some can be lifted and heeled in on a border (C). To protect heads of cauliflower and broccoli, from effects of rapid thaw after frost, take a spadeful of soil from the north side of plant, bend over head in that direction, heaping the soil over stem on opposite side (B).

Take care the spade or fork does not injure roots when lifting beet. Do not pull at the leaves; ease the root gently so that it comes from soil freely. Do not cut leaves, always twist them off as near crown as possible. Injured skin or cut leaves will cause beet to 'bleed.' Roots will deteriorate if exposed too long. Store them by covering with sand and sacking in boxes placed in a frost-proof shed.

When seedling wallflowers are transplanted 9 in. apart in rows 15 in. apart on the reserve border, pinch off the end of the tap root to produce good bushy plants. If those in the nursery bed are extra vigorous, with soft, sappy foliage, insert the fork 6 in. at the side, lift the plant until you hear a snap; this is the tap root breaking. It will help to produce more root fibres. Make soil firm on withdrawing fork.

When gladiolus leaves turn colour, lift and place them under cover for a week. Remove soil, cut off the stems about ½ in. above the corms, take off the old corm below the new, and save the small offset corms to plant in boxes of peat in spring. Store the main new corms in boxes or paper bags in a cool, frost-proof place with a little dry sand over them. They will keep perfectly in this way until planting time.

After begonias have finished flowering lift from beds and plant in boxes of sandy soil in the greenhouse. When foliage is dead remove it, shake corms free of soil, allow to dry, then store in boxes between layers of coconut fibre, silver sand or dry soil. Before bringing pot-plants into the greenhouse clear drainage holes of soil and scrub pots. Thoroughly clean the greenhouse too, before placing these plants under cover again.

When finally earthing up celery leave only 6 in. of foliage exposed, making the steep banking sides flat. Cover tops of ridges with straw or bracken to guard against frost. Leeks may be left in the ground during winter, lifting them as required. Use the hoe now constantly along the rows, drawing some soil up towards the stems. This increases the length of blanched stems; still greater length is obtained by tying leaves loosely, adding more soil as growth progresses. Avoid trapping overhanging leaf-tips, or the leeks will become deformed.

When harvesting the turnip crop, cut back the leaves and then, with a sharp knife, cut off the crowns of the plants. Prepare boxes of good leaf-mould and plant the crowns close together in this. Put the boxes in a warm, dark shed. Never allow the soil to get dry. In a few weeks' time long white leaf-stalks on which are small white leaves, will have grown, making a very good vegetable dish when cooked.

By forking the bed on which the turnips have been harvested, adding 3 oz. bonemeal per square yard if the soil is light, then treading and raking to make a fine seed bed, a sowing of Green Top Stones or Green Globe in drills 1 in. deep, 1 ft. apart, will produce a crop of turnip tops for use from January to March. Sprinkle superphosphate of lime when seedlings appear. A week later, and every three weeks after, give a dressing of old soot.

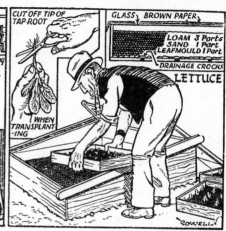

Between lifting and sowing crops, your soil may need nourishment. Animal manures being scarce, green-manuring is a good substitute. This consists of forking and raking the ground when a crop is lifted and then sowing quick-growing crops such as vetch tares, mustard or rape, 1 oz. per square yard. Don't sow the last two where cabbage or turnip have been growing previously. Dig in the crops and at the same time apply 2 oz. sulphate of ammonia per square yard: The decomposed plants provide humus, enabling light soils to retain moisture and heavy soils to become more friable.

The flavour of endive is too strong for use in its natural state, but when blanched it is excellent. By tying outer leaves, the heart goes white similarly to cos lettuce, but a better way is to cover each plant with an inverted plate, pot or box, according to the type grown, curled or Batavian. The broad-leafed variety will need a loose tie. Leave the covers on till blanching is complete. Transplant August-raised seedlings to a frame now for a winter supply; blanch them by covering the frame.

For a supply of lettuces during winter sow thinly in well-drained seed-boxes, prepared as shown, the compost being finely sifted. A few hours beforehand pour boiling water over the soil to sterilise it. When sown, sprinkle silver sand over the surface. Keep boxes covered until three or four leaves have formed, transplant to a bed in greenhouse at 9 in. apart or at 6 in. apart in other boxes. When replanting, snip off the tip of the tap root to help recovery on removal. Don't damage the tiny roots when planting.

When tidying up, one of the first things to be tackled is the clearing of fallen leaves. Use a birch broom for this, first shortening any twigs which are unduly long (inset A). Spread the twigs out fan-shape before using, and do not use an old, worn broom. Hold the broom nearly parallel to the ground, making long sweeps to cover as wide an area as possible.

Do not use a spade or fork to gather leaves. Use instead a pair of boards, held as shown in the inset. A single board can be used to rake in the leaves to a sack held open in the other hand. By using these methods, leaves are not so liable to blow away as they are when using a spade or fork. Use a wooden rake for clearing fallen leaves from the lawn and flower-beds. Rake them into piles and gather as shown.

Soft garden rubbish, lawn mowings and leaves form manure when rotted. Stack in a corner or bury it, sprinkling each layer with lime or salt to prevent smell. Small leaves buried in a pit will decay and form leaf-mould. Keep the pit covered and the leaves dry and they will be useful for making a hot-bed either used alone and compressed, or mixed with fresh manure. Place the frame on the bed, which must be 2 ft. deep. Later, the spent material can be usefully dug into the soil.

As farmyard manure is difficult to obtain, the garden compost heap makes a good substitute, and, with very little trouble, provides a constant source of home-made manure to be worked into the ground at digging time. If hop, poultry or a mixture of chemical manures is used in spring the results will prove almost as good as those produced by animal manure. In a sheltered corner dig a shallow pit into which put all kinds of vegetable material which will decay easily.

If a low concrete wall is made to enclose the heap it will make a neater job. In any case, the pit should not be too deep or fermentation will not be rapid or complete. A supply of air is necessary. A good plan is to divide the rubbish into soft green material, refuse of more fibrous growth, and that of a woody nature. Mix these by using double the quantity of soft material to that of coarser stuff.

Rotting is accelerated if the heap is made in 6 in. layers, as shown, using one of the reagents sold for the purpose instead of lime, and sulphate of ammonia, if desired. Turn the heap after one month, adding water. Then turn it again inside out a month later. Always keep it moist. Several materials which can be utilised in making up the heap are shown here. Hedge clippings, cabbage stalks and diseased plants should be burnt and not added to the heap.

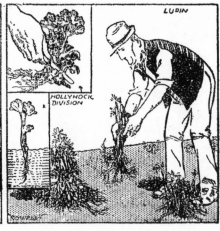

Various plants can be divided now to increase your stock. Lift kniphofia, or red-hot poker, carefully separate into pieces, replant where they are to grow, or pot and put in cold frame until rooted. Lift lily of the valley with a fork, pull apart, set the plants upright in a shallow trench 4 in. apart, and fill in, making soil firm. Give a mulch of sifted leaf-mould and decayed manure (inset A).

The day previous to lifting Michaelmas daisies soak the soil. Lift with a fork. Above the roots whitish crowns will be seen. Each clump is divided into five or six pieces, each containing about six crowns. The clumps are divided by pushing forks back to back into the clump and forcing handles apart. Choose the outside pieces, planting them 3 ft. apart, the crowns being 1 in. deep.

If violas are dug up, divided into several pieces and planted 4 in. apart, they will flower earlier than those raised by cuttings or seed. Take up carefully and shake off the soil of lupins, separate the clumps into divisions, thus making a separate plant of each. Hollyhocks, when lifted, consist of one or more crowns, with a number of plantlets around. Cut these away and replant them.

To prevent damage to plants in cold frames lay sacking over the glass at night when a frost is expected (inset A). Peg down or shorten long shoots of dwarf roses. If allowed to be blown about the soil becomes sodden at the stem base. Draw up the soil to the stem at the point where it was budded, and tie the branches together. Tie standards similarly and fasten straw round them (inset B).

Protect from frost bedding plants and those in cold greenhouses by draping them with sheets of newspaper. Place boards, kept in place with pegs, along rows of autumn-sown seedlings. On a severe night lay bracken or straw across them, removing it when danger is past. Place strawy manure over plantain lilies and peonies, and fibre over ranunculi and poppy anemones.

Pot-chrysanthemums should not suffer from frosty nights if newspaper is fixed over the supporting stakes, or if sacking is draped over a roughly made framework. Pampas grass and kniphofia (red-hot poker or torch lily) should have the foliage twisted and tied loosely, with leaves set round the base. Poppy anemones and ranunculus can be protected by bracken spread over the bed.

SPRING GREENS

DRAW SOIL UP TO STEMS OF YOUNG PLANTS

Covering of LITTER or DRY GRASS
3in. Square Lumps of SPAWN
Covering of Loamy SOIL
Compost ⅔ LEAVES, ⅓ LITTER

3½ ft.

MUSHROOMS

OVERLOOKING STORAGE

Space is saved when planting out late summer sowings of winter and spring greens by setting plants 9 in. apart in rows the same distance apart. Alternate rows (A and C in the diagram) may then be used when plants are large enough to cut, leaving rows 18 in. apart. Later, alternate plants in rows B and D can be cut. Remaining plants will then all be 18 in. apart; allow to develop fully before cutting them. The cabbage family must have an intermediate period in a nursery bed of well-dug soil in a sunny position. To avoid club-root, add 2 oz. per square yard of freshly slaked lime.

A crop of mushrooms is easily grown out of doors if you collect a large heap of fresh fallen leaves, some litter or dried grass, and loamy soil from below turves of grass. The bed can be as long as space allows, 3½ ft. at base and 3 ft. from base to flat ridge. Proportion of leaves should be two-thirds, and litter one-third. Firm the bed when settled, place the fresh loamy soil all over it to a depth of 3-in., and make firm with spade back. Into this press 3 in. square pieces of spawn 9 in. apart. Cover spawn with a 2-in. layer of loam. Make all firm and cover with 9-in. layer of dried grass.

It is advisable to look over your stored crops occasionally to see that all is well. Potatoes are successfully stored only if placed in darkness to prevent greening; they must be perfectly dry to prevent rot and there must be complete freedom from frost. Sacks or boxes are suitable storage places. To avoid troublesome development of disease sprinkle freshly slaked lime or flowers of sulphur among the tubers, using 2 oz. for an 8-stone sack. Dry rot causes them to become hard and useless; any found affected must be burned. Onions will keep longest when stored in a dry and airy shed.

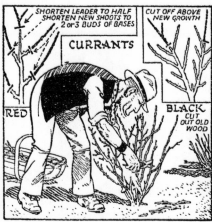

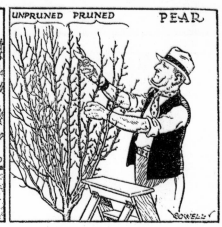

Red and white currants produce fruit buds on short spurs at the base of young shoots of current season's growth. Black currants yield fruit on shoots of previous season's growth; those developed this year will carry next season's fruit. New side shoots on red currants are cut back to within an inch or so of their bases. Leaders or terminals are shortened by about one-half. Young side shoots on black currants are not cut back. Old or unfruitful branches are cut out and others cut back to new growth.

Gooseberries produce fruit on short spurs all along the old branches and on sturdy new shoots. Shorten all thin, crowded and coarse-growing side shoots to within 1 in. of their bases. Cut to six buds medium-length shoots, and tip sturdy young shoots. Shorten by one-third good leader shoots, and weak ones by half. Always cut just above a plump bud. When dealing with old trees, aim to replace old growth with new. Cut away old branches year by year.

Pear trees (standard, bush, cordon, etc.) are pruned by cutting back side shoots of more than 5 in. or 6 in. to within three or four buds of their bases, and leaders are shortened by one-third or half, according to whether they are strong or weak. If a tree produces blossom, but not much fruit, shorten the longer spurs to half their length, and cut out some old spurs and new ones if they are crowded. Final results should leave spurs spaced at about 5 in. or 6 in, apart.

Soot is not soluble, but if placed in a bag suspended in a bucket of water the resulting soot water will contain valuable properties which have been extracted and is then useful as a fertiliser. Soot which has been kept in the open for a period can be forked around plants to keep pests away. When mixed with lime, it is a valuable deterrent to slugs.

The home-made scraper and cleaner will be found quite useful for gardening shoes. If the greenhouse is crowded just now portable hanging shelves for small pot-plants will give you extra space. Inset (A) is one of the bent copper wires having an eye at each end to go over nails driven into the sash bars (inset B).

Seed-boxes made of sheet zinc will last for years, and if varied sizes are made they will fit within each other for space-saving, when stored. Mark out a margin of 2½ in. Cut each corner along line X as shown, bend up the two ends and then the sides. Bend the protruding pieces round on to the ends and fix with rivets. Punch holes for drainage.

Fertility of your soil largely depends on the presence of lime. An easy way of testing whether your soil needs liming is to take several samples from your plot at a depth of 9 in. Mix these together, place a little in a tumbler, mix to a paste with a little water, then pour in a teaspoonful of spirits of salts. If effervescence ensues the soil contains enough lime; if not, it needs a dressing of about 6 oz. per sq. yd.

Lime improves both heavy and light soils; it renders heavy soil friable and light soil more compact. It sweetens all soils, is a plant-food and preventive of wireworms, other pests and club-root disease. Fork the lime into the top soil or scatter it and allow rain to wash it in. Quicklime, more useful on new ground, is slaked as shown. Apply lime in autumn on light soil and manure in spring; apply lime in spring on heavy soil and manure in autumn.

One of the best forms of humus is decayed leaves, especially small kinds, such as oak and beech. Large kinds and evergreens are useless for making leaf-mould; they should be burned, and the valuable ash used. Leaves are stored in a pit, heaped in the open, or dug into the ground. When heaped; a supply of rich leaf-mould is available by the end of a year. For potting composts, the leaves must be heaped for at least a year.

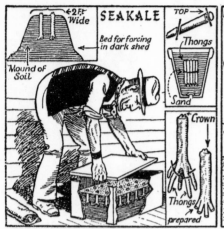

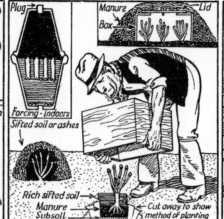

Roots of seakale can be forced into growth indoors or outdoors. For the former, a dark, warm shed or cellar is suitable. Lift main root with crown on top and trim off smaller pieces (thongs). Use these for propagating early in the year. To distinguish the tops from the bottoms of the thongs at a glance when planting time arrives, cut tops off horizontally and the other ends in a slanting direction. Tie thongs in bundles and store in pots of sand. Plant main roots a few inches apart, in covered boxes of soil kept moist.

The boxes can be put under the greenhouse staging from which sacking is hung. They may also be planted in large pots covered by others inverted. The young shoots are ready for cutting when 6 in. long. Instead of lifting seakale, boxes or large pots surrounded with fresh manure placed over the undisturbed roots will provide a supply of forced growth. These plants will last several years, whereas those lifted and forced are useless after.

Tall plants of brussels sprouts and those in exposed positions will need some support. Insert a stake at each end of the row and tie two or three lengths of strong string to each to keep the plants from being blown over. Take care when gathering the sprouts to avoid damaging the top clump of leaves. Gather lower sprouts first, a few from each plant. Remove all decaying leaves.

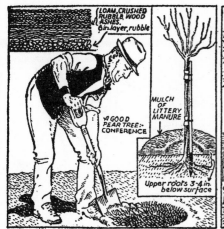

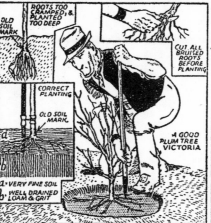

Now is the best time to plant pear, plum and apple trees. Choose a sheltered position on the north or east side of the garden for pears. Deep well-drained loam suits pears; light sand and heavy clay do not. Break up subsoil to a depth of 2 ft in a 4-ft. circle for each tree, placing a layer of rubble at the bottom if the soil is heavy. Plant pyramid and bush trees 10 ft. apart, espaliers against wall or fence 12 ft., and single cordons 2 ft.

Plum trees do best in light soil containing lime, sunny position, against wall or fence facing south or east. Plant at same depth as they were previously growing, as shown by the old soil mark; deep planting causes stunted growth. Pack fine soil around the spread roots, treading firmly. Do not put manure in the hole or against roots. Set supporting stakes before roots are covered.

Dwarf compact bush and single cordon apple trees are most suitable for small gardens; plant the first 9 ft. apart, single cordons 2 ft. apart. Dig deeply and prepare soil as shown for each tree. Place a mulch of manure to cover a 3-ft. circle round each tree, leaving the manure to decay on surface. Apply sulphate of potash in the spring at the rate of 3 to 4 oz. per square yard.

By preparing and planting the herbaceous border now earlier progress will be made. Dig the soil 20 in. (two spade-blade depths). Enrich the lower soil with manure, and the upper with bonemeal or basic slag. Place the plants, which should be labelled, with a view to advantageous display, both as to height and colour grouping. The colour chart on page 115 will help you in the last-mentioned case.

Shoots about 9 in. long cut from the past summer's growth on flowering shrubs, planted in a 6-in. deep narrow trench on a sheltered border will root by spring. Make the trench with sloping back, scattering sand in the bottom. Prepare the shoots by cutting just below a joint. Press soil firmly at the base of each, not at the top. Set them 6 in. apart, the trenches being 1 ft. from each other.

If you wish to force seakale, chicory or rhubarb, lift and place the roots in boxes of soil in a cellar or beneath the greenhouse staging; in the latter case, mats should be hung in front of them to keep them in darkness. Rhubarb left in ground should have leaves removed, given a mulch of manure and some ashes heaped over the corms. Early in the new year some of these can be forced, as shown on page 11.

If space in your garden is limited, the best type of apple or pear tree to buy is the single cordon, and grow it obliquely. This tends to check the upward flow of sap, thus helping to form side fruit buds. When grown at a good angle, a longer fruiting stem is possible and sunshine is able to reach the lowest part. Cordons may be used as a division of one part of the garden from another or alongside a path.

At each end of the prepared row dig a hole 2 ft. deep in which strong posts are fixed, embedding them in concrete. When this has set hard, wires are stretched 2 ft. apart between the posts. Canes 8 ft. long are then secured to the wires at a good angle, spacing them at about 2 ft. apart. Planting is then done in soil prepared as shown in the inset. Tie the trees to the canes at intervals.

Plant single fruit trees in holes 3 ft. in diameter, two spits deep. Loosen subsoil, which should then be trodden and sufficient top soil replaced so that the upper roots are two or three inches below surface. Where scion and stock join should be at soil level. Spread roots out before planting, cutting back any damaged. Tread soil around stems after planting. Supporting stakes should be driven in before refilling holes.

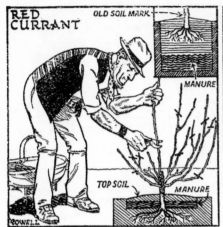

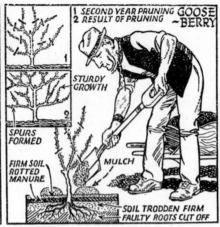

Plant red currant bushes now; those three years old are best. Dig deeply, adding old manure, wood-ash, etc. Pack the spread roots with fine soil, upper roots being covered with 2 or 3 in. of trodden soil. Spread a manure mulch around each bush. Cut back main shoots to about half length after planting, and badly placed ones to two or three buds of their base. Cut all laterals to within 1 in. of their base on established bushes; cut young leaders at branch ends to about half their length. After pruning, dig in manure just below surface.

All gardens should have a few gooseberry bushes. Plant them 4½ ft. apart any time from now till mid-March in well-tilled soil. Before planting, dig in wood ash, leafmould, manure, etc., and fork in ½ lb. basic slag per square yard. Plant firmly but not deeply, as shown. Prune a few weeks later, weak shoots to half length, strong ones to within two or three buds of their base. Shorten crowded side shoots of established bushes, merely tipping good young shoots and the leading shoot extending main branches by one-third.

When pruning, select good, straight cuttings of either of these bush fruits for propagation. Remove all buds but the top four or five to prevent suckers being thrown up. Cut any unripe wood from the top and the base close below a joint. Set the cuttings in a narrow straight-backed trench 6 in. deep, gooseberry cuttings 6 in. apart, red currants 9–12 in. Press sand or sandy soil round the bases, fill in and tread firm. See that they are not loosened by frost.

Roses should be planted this month unless the ground is sodden or frozen. The soil should be prepared a few days previously, digging about 20 in. deep, keeping the layers in their original positions. The treatment for chalk, sandy or clay soil is seen in the insets. Cut back all bruised and broken root-ends, and shorten those without fibres (inset A).

Do not plant roses too deeply. Bush and dwarf kinds should be set so that the place at which the tree was budded is only an inch or so below the surface. Dig wide enough for roots to be spread, making the centre of the hole higher than the edge. The upper roots need only be covered by two or three inches of soil.

Tar ends of stakes for standards and insert them before the roots are covered. Soil around the roots must be made firm; loose planting is useless. If it is not possible to plant when trees arrive, heel them in temporarily in a trench so that the roots are covered. Spread dry soil over roots if the ground is wet. If the weather is dry at planting time, water the trees in.

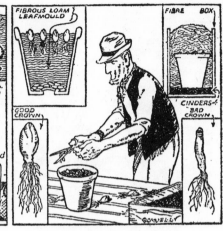

Plant beds of May-flowering Darwin and cottage tulips in well-drained sandy loam soil. Dig the ground over, scattering and forking in 2 oz. bonemeal per square yard. If decayed manure is used, it must be 10 in. below the surface. Use trowel or blunt dibber for planting, leaving no space below the bulbs, which should be set on sand about 4 in. below the surface, 6 in. apart.

Hyacinth bulbs should be heavy, firm and solid. If planting out of doors, use medium size rather than large. Details of planting both indoor and outdoor bulbs are shown in the insets. A dark, airy room is the best place for indoor culture, keeping the fibre moist. For outdoor culture, a sunny position with well-drained loamy soil is best.

Give a top-dressing of sifted leafmould and decayed manure in equal parts to the lily of the valley bed. Good single crowns having their roots shortened to one-third length can be placed, 1 in. apart, in 6-in. pots of loam and leaf-mould and made firm. Place pots on cinders in a box, covering with peat fibre, or in a cold frame covered with ashes till January.

A plot of ground not previously culti-vated, or old neglected land, can be made workable by first stripping it of rough grass and weeds. Divide the plot into strips. Each strip is cleared in turn, trimming off the rough growth with a grass hook (inset 1); stripping the top layer with a short-bladed grub-bing mattock, and raking off the rubbish before tackling the next section (inset 2).

The top layer of weeds and soil will probably be infested with pests. It should all be burned, the bonfire being added to as each section is cleared, resulting in a valuable topdressing, for later use. The turves of rough grass-land should be turned on the soil, grass-side downwards (3) and left. When dried out break them up into small pieces and dig them in (4).

If the soil of your new plot is heavy clay or is infested with pests divide it into strips two spits wide, running the way the ground slopes. Throw the soil up into ridges, working backwards from the first strip. These ridges expose as much surface as possible to the good effects of hard weather, so that by the spring the soil is in a friable working condition.

Bulbs in pots and bowls whose flowering period is over should be carefully stored under the benches of the greenhouse for replanting later. The crowns of rhubarb and seakale in boxes and pots should be packed round with leaves and manure and covered with inverted boxes or pots. Cut down chrysanthemum plants which have finished flowering to within a few inches of the base to make room for them to throw up shoots for cuttings.

Old fuchsia plants must be kept dry, the young plants only being watered. Pots in which cuttings are to be planted should be thoroughly washed with an insecticide and seed-boxes should be dipped in the same liquid. Plants need rest; the temperature in the greenhouse should be just sufficient to keep them safe from frost, and not great enough to encourage growth. Paper bag coverings at night are a useful protection.

If the berries of mistletoe are rubbed or pressed in crevices of the bark or clefts between branches of apple, willow, hawthorn, lime or poplar; the seeds will become established, the sticky substance surrounding the seeds enables them to keep in place. Do not cut the bark; wipe it with some old sacking. Turn over the leaf heap to promote decay. Woolly-leafed rockery plants can be covered with glass to protect them from rain.

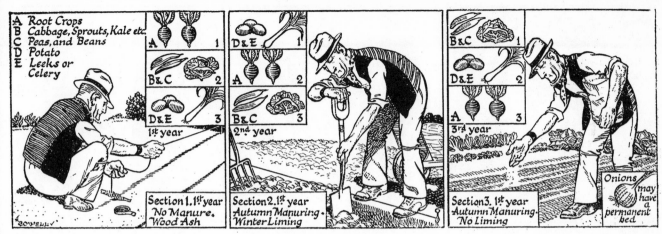

A Root Crops
B Cabbage, Sprouts, Kale etc.
C Peas, and Beans
D Potato
E Leeks or Celery

A 1
B&C 2
D&E 3
1st year

Section 1. 1st year
No Manure.
Wood Ash

D&E 1
A 2
B&C 3
2nd year

Section 2. 1st year
Autumn Manuring.
Winter Liming

B&C 1
D&E 2
A 3
3rd year

Section 3. 1st year
Autumn Manuring.
No Liming

Onions may have a permanent bed

If vegetables of the same 'family' are grown on the same soil season after season, underfeeding of the soil results. Some vegetables obtain their nourishment from the upper soil; others, deeper rooting, from the lower soil. If deep feeders follow shallow feeders, the top soil has time to recover the drain imposed on it by the previous crop. Some vegetables, by reason of the method of their cultivation, such as the earthing-up of celery and potatoes, clean the soil.

A wise plan is to mark out and divide your plot into sections. If it is small, three sections will do, allowing a permanent site for such crops as rhubarb, asparagus or seakale. Onions may also be grown on the same ground each season. As a general rule, roots should not follow roots, but carrots may follow turnips, for they belong to different 'families.' Don't forget to leave room for a seed bed.

The insets show how each type of vegetable has a change of ground each season for three years and is grown again on its original section the fourth year. In the same way the manuring and liming treatment of each section differs each season, so that by rotating these also, season after season, every part of the plot is limed once in three years, and each has a rest from animal or compost manurial treatment once in the same period.

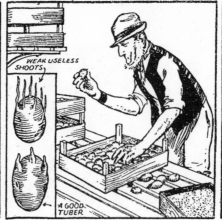

Protect Christmas rose from rain by placing moss around it, covering with a portable frame or handlight. Other plants needing similar treatment are auriculas, winter aconite (*Eranthis hyemalis*), *Primula winteri* and miniature irises. A 'collar' placed around these plants and a raised sheet of glass above them will save them from excessive wet.

Stored roots and tubers should be examined, and any which appear to be decaying should be discarded. Dahlia tubers which have only just started to rot may be saved by cutting the bad part away, drying the tubers, and liming the cut part. Rub off superfluous 'eyes' from seed tuber potatoes.

Clean and sharpen any tools needing attention. Rub them afterwards with an oily rag. Scrape any dirt from the spade; a clean tool means easier work. See that the blades of the shears fit close together. Any tools not needed for some time should be wrapped in paper or rag when oiled before being stored under cover.

Don't neglect to cut down hardy perennials to within a few inches of the ground. Don't dig up and divide clumps in the border if the soil is too wet. Don't allow refuse to accumulate; burn it as soon as possible. Don't omit to give fruit trees and shrubs a top dressing; the fruit trees will benefit by a forking of slaked lime around them.

Don't discard old fork and spade handles; cut to shape; they make good dibbers. Don't water cacti during the winter. Don't open root clamps in very frosty or wet weather. Don't neglect to burn any currant bushes showing big bud. Don't spread manure on beds during frost. Don't forget to heel over broccoli, so that frozen heads do not face the sun.

Don't forget to spread bracken leaves or litter along the celery ridges during bad weather. Don't allow the soil in violet beds in cold frames to become dry or allow runners, dead or decayed leaves. Don't omit to ventilate the frames freely when possible, to prevent plants from damping off. Don't fail to cover frames at night in severe weather.

Now is the time to prepare ground for future sowing and planting. A certain amount of digging is needed in every part of the garden each year; soil occupied by permanent plants and trees cannot, of course, be dug thoroughly, but it should be forked over. The food plot can be divided into three equal parts, one being mock trenched one year and the others plain dug, reversing the order the next year.

Divide the plot to be dug into strips about 1 ft. wide. Open the first strip 1 ft. deep, the excavated soil being removed to the other end of the plot. Into the empty trench turn the soil 1 ft. or spit deep from the next strip. This procedure is carried on till you have opened the last trench. This is filled with the soil taken from the first trench. Remember, if you are not used to digging, not to do too much at first.

When mock trenching, the second spit (D) is forked, and on it a 3-in. layer of manure, garden refuse, leaves or hop manure is placed. Then soil (A) from the adjoining strip is turned on it. Different treatment of light and heavy soil is shown in the insets. The earlier your soil is dug the longer period it has to benefit from frost, snow and wind. Heavy soils can be left rough; they will be more friable in the spring.

Whilst it is better to plant evergreen shrubs in spring or early autumn, the best period in which to plant the leaf-losing kinds is now whilst the growth is dormant. The hawthorn or may *(Cratægus)* is cheap, and grows quickly into a dense hedge. To grow a hedge successfully, see to drainage, trench the ground 2½ ft. wide along the site to a depth of 2 ft., breaking up the bottom. Prune them well back after the first year.

Partly fill trench with manure, replacing some of the soil to top level. Put plants in 1 ft. apart in a double row, those in one row opposite spaces in the other. Cut plants back at time of planting, which should be when mild and the ground not sodden. If hawthorns get thin at base, hoe the weeds, partly cut through stems near base, bend them down, tying to stakes along the hedge line. New shoots will start near ground, filling the hedge gaps.

Apart from low-growing plants, edgings to paths and borders can be made by placing two boards held in position by bricks, filling the space with a mixture of cement and stones: removing bricks and board when the concrete is fairly firm, replacing them along the line for the next section, and so on. Bricks embedded either slanting, set flat, or flat and upright alternately, make a good edging. Large stones or tiles are other forms of successful edgings.

Winter spraying of fruit trees with a tar-oil wash kills both insects and their eggs, lichen and moss. Before spraying, complete the winter pruning. Spray before buds have started into growth. The spray nozzle, kept on the move, should be held close to the tree, taking care to cover all sides of all branches. Any vegetables or plants growing beneath the trees should be covered while spraying, as the liquid will scorch the leaves.

Fruit bushes, particularly gooseberries, need protection from birds, as they may peck the newly forming buds. A small-mesh netting cover will do this, or the bushes may be enveloped in black thread, wound from branch to branch. By clipping the thread reel to a stick, the thread may be played out similarly to the line on a fishing rod. Another method is to spray the bushes with lime sulphur or a quassia wash. If rain follows, give a second spray.

Winter pruning of apples, etc., while the trees are dormant can be carried out until March. The short woody spurs formed along main branches are helped by shortening young lateral shoots to within two or three buds of the base of previous growth. Cut out unhealthy shoots. Shorten all laterals that are over 4 in. long. The terminal growth at the branch top is shortened by about one-third its length, or, if weakly, by half. Cut to a bud pointing the way you wish it to extend.

PLANNING NEW GARDENS

You may have moved to a new house, or the repairs to your present building may be nearing completion. The builder has probably left you an untidy plot which you hope eventually to convert into a garden of beauty and usefulness. Before starting the actual work on the spot, it will pay in the long run to do a spot of work on paper.

Take measurements of boundaries; note the aspect to determine which part of the garden will get the most sunshine. Make a plan on paper of the general shape of the plot. Work out, with no undue haste, the general lay-out of paths, lawn, flower-beds and borders, the vegetables garden, the best positions for planting fruit trees and bushes, for the setting of bird-bath, sundial or seat. Perhaps a paved or sunken garden and pond may be worked into the scheme.

The plot may be small, but, even so, it will probably present many possibilities after careful consideration. If any trees have been allowed to remain don't decide in haste to do away with them; a tree can often be both useful and ornamental.

Next dig a few holes about 1½ ft. in depth to determine the nature of the soil, whether it is waterlogged, light or heavy. Light soils are mainly of sandy composition and do not retain moisture. They, therefore, need plenty of heavy manure. Heavy soils need gritty substances and strawy manure to keep the fine soil particles more open.

Do not make paths narrower than is necessary. Paths should always have a purpose, leading to an ornament, the kitchen garden, the tool shed, etc.

Do not set tall-growing trees or a trellis too near the house. They will reduce the light in the rooms and obstruct your view into the garden. A climber-covered trellis makes a useful screen to conceal the kitchen garden. Don't cramp a small garden by crowding it with borders crossing the view; arrange the beds in lines running from the house.

On the other hand, aim at creating hidden nooks and corners full of unexpected charm. The diagrams in the following pages may help by suggesting to you some ideas in the planning of a new garden or ways by which to improve your existing plot. The sizes and shapes of the various parts will be governed by the amount of ground you have. They can be modified to suit your needs.

If you choose a plan to work on, some alteration of crops may be necessary according to whether your garden faces north or south, east or west. Should it adjoin older property, the question of established trees overhanging the plot may necessitate slight alteration of layout; therein the interest lies.

AN 'ALL-IN' BACK GARDEN

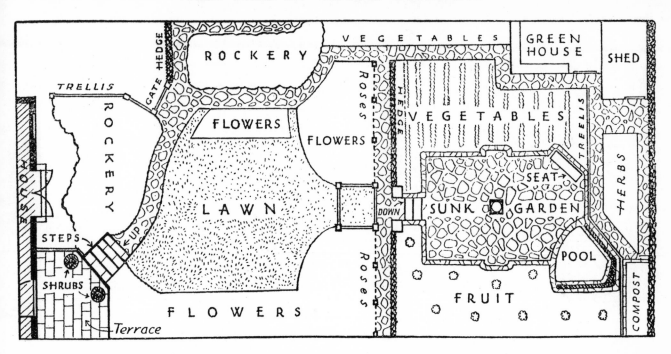

Box trees in tubs on a paved terrace stand at the head of steps leading down to a path skirting the lawn, with two rockeries on the left. Across the lawn the sunk garden, with seat and pool, is visible from the house, while the vegetable and fruit plots are hidden by a hedge. Tool shed, herb garden and compost heap are placed behind a trellis across the end of the vegetable, fruit and sunk gardens.

ANOTHER ATTRACTIVE AND PRACTICAL BACK GARDEN

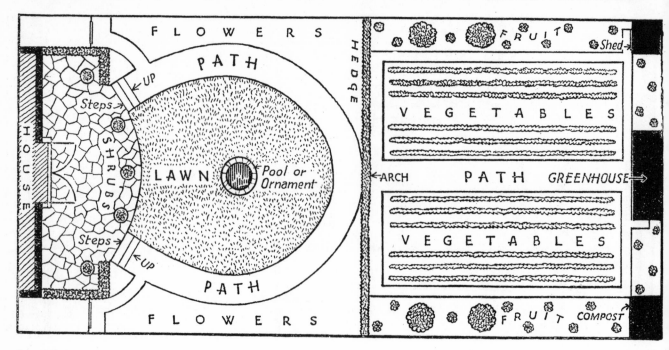

Beyond the crazy-paved terrace, steps lead down to paths skirting the horse-shoe shaped lawn, in the centre of which stands a pool or ornament. The pathway continues under an arch in the hedge, which cuts off the view of the vegetable garden, to the greenhouse, shed and compost heap. Fruit is planted on either side of the vegetable plots. Each part is reached by paths.

A MORE ELABORATE LAYOUT

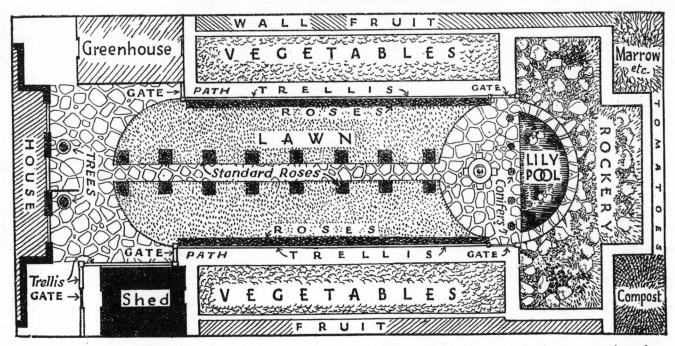

The pathway down the centre of a long narrow lawn, edged with standard rose trees, leads to a paved garden and lilypool. This is backed by a large rockery. Hidden by roses on a trellis, the vegetable and fruit gardens are placed on either side of the lawn and are reached by gates. The greenhouse, at the house end of the garden, hides the vegetables on one side, while on the opposite side the tool shed serves the same purpose and is shut off by a trellis.

SIMPLE BUT ATTRACTIVE

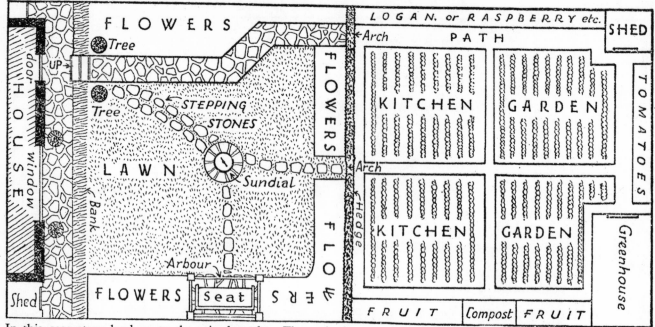

In this case steps lead up to the raised garden. Flower-beds are made on three sides of the lawn, across which stepping-stones are placed. From a sundial in the centre of the lawn one set of stones leads to an arbour seat, the other to an arch in the hedge which screens the kitchen garden. The crazy paving ends at another arch, from which the path continues as a gravel walk alongside the wall fruit and kitchen garden. Tool shed and greenhouse are at the end of the garden.

As mentioned in the Foreword, if this garden faced a southern aspect, the tomato bed would have to be moved to the front of the hedge. The seat, too, would probably be better on the other side of the lawn.

110

NEW SUGGESTIONS FOR YOUR FRONT GARDEN

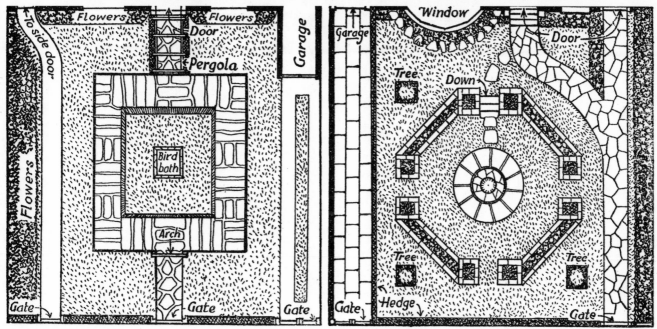

This design for a front garden shows the path from the front gate, passing around a squared sunken lawn with bird-bath in the centre, to the porch, before which there is a pergola. A lawn surrounds the path. To the left of this is the path to the side door, with a flower-bed bordering it.

Low brick walls on the lawn enclose flower-beds surrounding a lower inner part of the lawn, in the centre of which stands a circular paving to set off a garden ornament. This is joined to the main lawn by grass slopes on three sides and steps and stones on the fourth. A rockery is built in front of the window,

MORE IDEAS FOR FRONT GARDENS

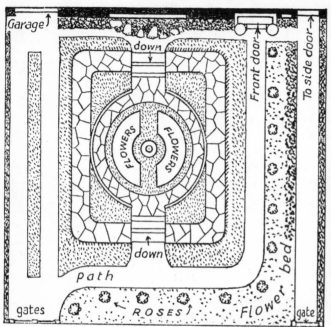

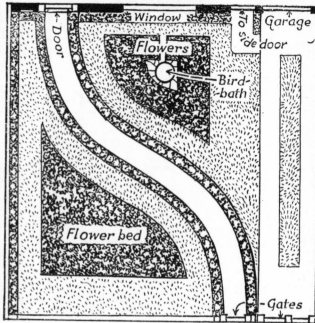

On the right of the path from the gates to the front door rose trees stand along the edge of a flower-bed. On the left of the path a narrow strip of lawn surrounds a path with steps on two sides leading down to a small sunken flower garden, with a central bird-bath. A grass strip breaks up the runway to the garage.

Here the curved path to the front door is flanked by a narrow flower border which continues in front of the window and along the left side of the garden. A shaped flower-bed stands in each half of the lawn. On the one near the window a bird-bath stands on a similarly shaped paving, a small path joining it with the lawn.

SUGGESTIONS FOR SPRING FLOWER-BEDS—

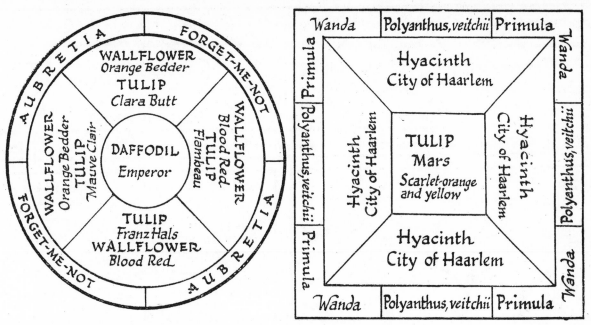

When preparing spring beds dig in plenty of material from the compost heap, but use no fresh manure. Give a dressing of lime, 4 oz. per square yard. Bulbs should be planted with a groundwork of dwarfer plants, which not only set off the flowers of the bulbs but afford them support. Think out a definite colour-scheme before you start any planting. Get the groundwork and edging plants in first. Wallflowers, forget-me-nots, aubretia, double white *Arabis* all make settings to May-flowering tulips. A mass of one of the giant trumpet daffodils in the centre of a bed, as shown here, is very effective. In a bed of hyacinths surrounded by a border a central group of scarlet or orange tulips is charming. Many beautiful schemes are possible on similar lines.

—AND THREE FOR MIXED SUMMER BEDS

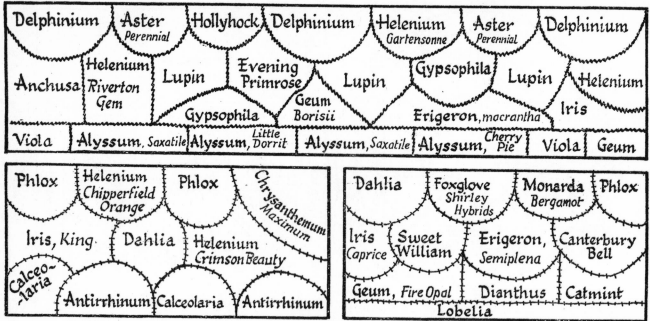

Plans are shown here of suggestions for three mixed summer flower borders. A combination of herbaceous plants with biennials will enable the beds to make good colour effects throughout early and late summer. When deciding on the placing of such subjects as dahlias, heleniums, etc., consideration must be given to varieties in each case in accordance with their maximum height. Tallest kinds are, of course, planted at the back of the border. Other suggestions for summer beds are two kinds of antirrhinums, tall and intermediate, with an edging of dwarf nasturtiums; cheiranthus, calendula, with white alyssum as an edging; Canterbury bell, mixed colours, with *Ageratum*, imperial dwarf blue, in the front of the bed.

COLOUR HARMONY IN THE GARDEN

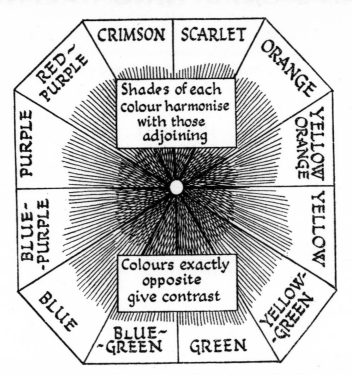

CRIMSON SCARLET
ORANGE
RED-PURPLE
PURPLE
YELLOW ORANGE
BLUE-PURPLE
YELLOW
BLUE
YELLOW-GREEN
BLUE-GREEN GREEN

Shades of each colour harmonise with those adjoining

Colours exactly opposite give contrast

Garden beds and borders should be planned, as far as possible, with a view to attaining colour harmony and contrast. The colours in this chart are arranged in such a way that the tones, whether light or dark, of one colour combine harmoniously with the tones of the colour in the next or near section.

Colours in sections of the diagram opposite to each other will form a vivid contrast. When arranging plants in the bed aim at obtaining harmony with a few striking contrasts rather than getting many contrasts and few harmonies.

Another point to bear in mind when planning flower-beds is that flowers of some colours prefer brilliant sunshine while others like shade or semi-shade. As a rough rule, the brighter the tones the greater the need for sun. Flowers of more delicate pastel shades prefer cooler positions.

ADAM'S GARDENING CALENDAR

What to do each month in the year

The numbers refer to illustrated pages

JANUARY

Flower Garden.   Loosen soil around visible bulbs. Dust with 1 oz. superphosphate per square yard.

Protect crocuses from birds with stretched black thread.

Protect autumn-sown annuals, roses, poppy anemone, ranunculus, pampas grass and red-hot poker from frost, 9.

Burn all wood garden rubbish.

Pinch out tops of 'leggy' wallflowers; remove dead leaves. Dress with lime, 13.

Make rock gardens, 15.

Lift, divide and replant edging pinks.

Sow, in sheltered corners, Shirley poppy, Virginia stock, cornflower.

Top-dress rhododendrons and azaleas, 13.

Fruit Garden.   Winter-prune fruit trees, 14. Winter-spray fruit trees with a tar-oil wash.

Fork between all fruit trees and bushes.

Kitchen Garden. Destroy pests, 12.

Sow early peas; lettuce, 16; carrot and broad beans.

Level and rake old celery beds.

Cover rhubarb for early supply, 11.

Plant horseradish and Jerusalem artichokes.

Dress heavy soil with lime, and light soils with ground chalk.

Protect broccoli hearts from frost by bending the leaves over them.

Top dress asparagus beds with well-rotted manure.

Examine stored root crops, and remove any which show signs of decay.

Under Glass. Make hot-beds, 10.

Dig up rhubarb roots and set in boxes for forcing, 11.

Take chrysanthemum cuttings.

Remove rooted bulbs in plunged pots to frame.

Pot lily-of-the-valley roots.

Sow half-hardy annuals : antirrhinums, petunias, verbena, French marigold, salpiglossis, zinnia, *ageratum* and lobelia for summer bedding.

Sow onions, tomatoes and lettuces in seed pans or boxes.

Make a sowing of sweet peas.

Flower Garden. Spike lawn with fork; rake and apply lime.

Plant dwarf Michaelmas daisies.

Give basic slag dressing to roses, Canterbury bells, sweet-williams.

Top-dress lilies.

Sow calendula, 21.

Sprinkle weathered soot around polyanthuses and forget-me-nots.

Prepare bed and sow sweet peas, 21.

Start planting gladioli, 24.

Plant alpines, 19.

Divide catmint, replant 6–9 in. apart.

Transplant seedling perennials.

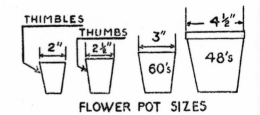

FLOWER POT SIZES

Fruit Garden. Dress strawberry bed with basic slag, 4 oz. per square yard, and make new beds, 20.

Watch for canker, 20.

Feed all fruit with artificial manure.

Plant outdoor grape vïnes.

Cut down autumn-fruiting raspberries and remove tips of summer-fruiting raspberries.

Kitchen Garden. Dig green pea, celery and leek trenches, 22.

Prepare onion bed, 18.

Sow early carrots, 18.

Stand seed potatoes in shallow boxes in a light, frost-proof place for sprouting.

Sow parsnips near the end of the month.

FLOWER POT SIZES

6"
8½"
9½"
24's
32's
16's

NUMBERS REPRESENT QUANTITY IN CAST

Under Glass. Start begonia and gloxinia tubers into growth, 17.

Take pelargonium (geranium) cuttings.

Take cuttings of fuchsias, 17; petunias, lobelia, perpetual carnations.

Repot ferns, 23.

Prevent damping-off of geraniums. Remove dead leaves of these and of violets.

Sow aquilegias, kochia, *Phlox drummondii*, tobacco flower.

Start dahlias into growth.

Sow carrots in frame.

Sow early salad crops in frames.

Sow celery and leeks.

Pot up lilies.

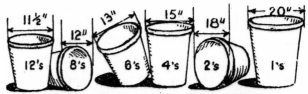

11½"
12"
13"
15"
18"
20"
12's
8's
6's
4's
2's
1's

POTS ARE SOLD UNDER NUMBER

MARCH

Flower Garden. Fork lightly and manure borders.

Water delphiniums with sulphate of iron, ½ oz. per gallon.

Overhaul the rock garden.

Sow hardy annuals.

Plant herbaceous perennials.

Give irises nitrate of soda, 1 oz. per square yard.

Plant lilies, 30.

Start rose pruning at the end of the month, 32.

Propagate lupin and delphiniums by shoot cuttings.

Propagate Michaelmas daisies by cutting and replanting young rooted growths.

Give rose beds a dressing of hop manure.

Make miniature rock gardens in troughs, 28.

Fruit Garden. Dress fruit trees with superphosphate, 4 oz. per square yard.

Fork and mulch strawberry plants.

Kitchen Garden. Plant shallots, early potatoes and sow early peas, 26.

Sow lettuce, 27; and radish, 27.

Plant out onions, 31. Plant glass-raised broad beans.

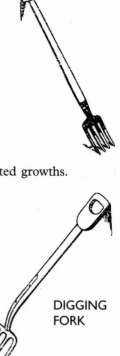

DIGGING FORK

Protect seedlings, especially peas, from birds, 26.

Divide rhubarb crowns and make new beds.

Sow brussels sprouts.

Pinch out broad bean suckers.

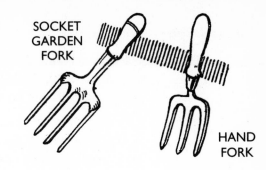

SOCKET GARDEN FORK

HAND FORK

Under Glass. Sow mustard and cress.

Repot plants needing treatment, 25.

Prick out crowded seedlings into other boxes.

When bulb flowers fade put pots in frames until foliage withers.

Sow french beans in boxes for forcing; also turnip and shorthorn carrots.

Sow maize.

Sow asters and ten-week stocks.

Sow primulas.

Sow vegetable marrow at latter part of month.

Sow celery for main crop in light soil.

Sow half-hardy annuals in frame.

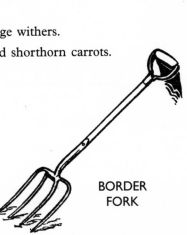

BORDER FORK

Flower Garden. Plant out sweet peas, 34; also violas, pansies, antirrhinums, carnations.

Spray roses at the first sign of green-fly.

Feed lily-of-the-valley with weak soot water.

Clip evergreens, and prune flowering shrubs, 36.

Plant evergreens, 36.

Take cuttings of aucuba, 36.

Sow biennials and perennials in nursery bed.

Lift bulbs as leaves fade. Dry and store when growth ends.

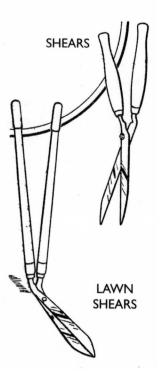

SHEARS

LAWN SHEARS

Fruit Garden. Graft shoots on to cut-back branches, 35.

Spray strawberry plants, 37, and dress beds with bonemeal.

Spray fruit trees and bushes.

Kitchen Garden. Overhaul the herb garden, 33.

Plant seakale and sow kohl-rabi, 37.

Plant asparagus bed, 38.

Plant second early and main crop potatoes.

Sow broccoli, 39.

Thin out seedlings.

Stake peas needing support.

Prepare marrow beds.

Sow french beans towards end of month.

Under Glass. Take cuttings of border chrysanthemums.

Sow celeriac on a hot-bed, 39.

Prick out half-hardy annuals sown in February.

Sow runner beans in boxes.

Sow ridge cucumbers and melons.

Repot azaleas that have flowered.

Sow cinerarias for winter flowering.

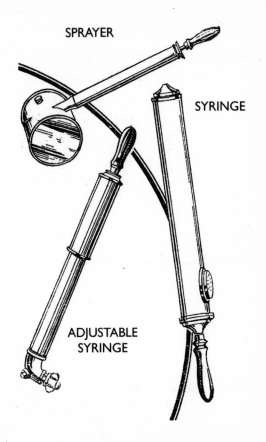

SPRAYER

SYRINGE

ADJUSTABLE
SYRINGE

MAY

Flower Garden. Plant out hardy bedding plants.

Divide rock plants when blooms have faded.

Take up tulips where necessary, 46.

Plant out nemesia, cosmos, kochia, salpiglossis, 46.

Support plants that need it, 46.

Get rid of rose suckers.

Plant out heliotrope at the end of month.

Mulch and disbud roses, 48.

Dress the lawn, 48.

Fruit Garden. Prune Morello cherries.

Reduce the number of runners on strawberry plants.

Bark-ring fruit trees of vigorous growth, 45.

Look out for woolly aphis, 45.

Kitchen Garden. Plant outdoor tomatoes, 43; and marrows.

Keep carrot-flies away, 47. Spray with liquid derris

against black-fly on beans and other crops.

SWAN-NECKED HOE

TRIANGULAR HOE

POTATO HOE

DUTCH HOE

RIVETED HOE

ONION HOE

MAY *(continued)*

Plant out savoy and cauliflowers, 47.

Sow another row of peas; support those growing with twiggy
  sticks.

Prepare celery trenches, and sow lettuces on the ridges.

Pinch out the tops of broad beans.

Continue to thin out seedlings of onions, carrots, etc.

Hoe freely between the crops.

Plant out leeks.

Under Glass.

Sow ridge cucumbers, 41; and plant frame cucumbers, 41.

Prick out celery seedlings.

Plant indoor tomatoes, 43.

Water pot-plants, 48.

Harden off bedding plants.

Sow pansies.

Arum lilies can be placed out-of-doors for the summer at the end of the month.

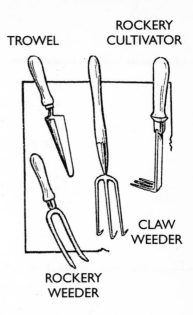

TROWEL

ROCKERY CULTIVATOR

CLAW WEEDER

ROCKERY WEEDER

JUNE

Flower Garden. Prune early blooming shrubs: mock orange, weigela, spirea, deutzia and lilac.

Uproot the suckers growing at bases of lilac.

Take measures to destroy pests on roses, 49.

Sow Canterbury bell and *Coreopsis* and many hardy plants on a reserve border.

Plant out dahlias, 53.

Rid lawn of daisies and plantains, 53.

Pick off seed-pods of rhododendrons and azaleas.

Restrict sweet peas to one or two stems, 54.

Trap ants, 56.

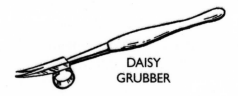

DAISY GRUBBER

Fruit Garden. Spray against aphis on fruit trees.

Reduce number of fruits in clusters on trees bearing heavy crops.

Don't allow fruit trees against walls to become dry. Shorten their side shoots to within six leaves of current year's growth.

Kitchen Garden. Cease cutting asparagus after the third week this month.

Make a final sowing of peas and french beans.

Spray late potatoes with Burgundy mixture against blight.

Plant out brussels sprouts, 50.

Check maggots of onion-fly, 50.

Plant out maize, 50; celery, 53.

Distinguish between friends and foes of the garden, 56.

Stop marrows when leading shoots are 2 ft. long, 54.

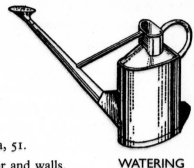

WATERING
CAN

Under Glass. Make successive sowings of fairy primrose and calceolaria, 51.

Ventilate greenhouse freely, shade roof glass, moisten floor and walls.

Propagate hydrangeas, 55.

Take cuttings of pansies and violas, 55.

Don't allow soil around tomatoes to become sodden; keep the house cool when plants are in bloom.

Place dormant bulbs in pots on their sides in a frame.

Pot chrysanthemums finally, 51.

Thin the vine and dust with flowers of sulphur, 51.

JULY

Flower Garden. Bud roses, 57.

Sow hollyhock, snapdragon, gaillardia, anchusa, foxglove on reserve border.

Layer carnations and pinks, 60.

Allow some plants, such as aquilegia and lupin, to mature for seed saving.

Sow at once after gathering seed.

Prune orange ball buddleia.

Fruit Garden. Layer strawberries, 60.

Cut off and burn branches on plum trees attacked by silverleaf.

Summer-prune apple and pear trees, leaving leaders uncut until winter.

Prune raspberries and look for reversion on black currants, 62.

Kitchen Garden. Mulch vegetables, 58. Trap slugs, 58.

Take measures to cure mildew on tomatoes, 61.

Lift shallots, 64. Sow spring cabbages, radish and parsley, 64.

Pinch out side shoots on tomato plants. Feed as soon as small fruits form.

Check for 'blisters' on celery, 62.

Plant out leeks, 64.

Sow turnip seed to provide roots in autumn.

Sow parsley for winter use.

Collect and dry herbs.

Sow endive and lettuce.

Sow spring cabbage.

North – beginning of month.

South – towards the end.

HAND CULTIVATOR

Under Glass.   Propagate fleshy-leaved plants by leaf cuttings, 59.

Propagate, by pieces of root, anchusa, iris, bouvardia, oriental poppy,

paeony, Japanese anemone, 59.

Attend to tomato plants affected by stripe or mildew, 61.

Set rambler rose cuttings in glass jars of water; pot when rooted.

Repot old corms of Persian cyclamen in cold frame.

Pot freesia bulbs in sandy loam in cold frame until rooted.

Prick out cinerarias.

Sow stocks for winter flowering.

Sow freesia seed thinly for flowering in spring.

AUGUST

Flower Garden   Plant colchicum, 70. Persian cyclamen, squill, autumn crocus, winter aconite.

Chionodoxa, 70; snowdrop, 66; belladonna lily.

Sow pot marigolds.

Sow on reserve border eschscholtzia, cornflower, nigella, larkspur, scabious, Shirley poppy, 65.

Prune rambler roses, 65. Take cuttings of yew, 65.

Clip evergreen hedges, 65; and other evergreens.

Attend to mildew on roses, 68.

Renovate lawns, 68.

Plant eranthis, 70. Plant bulb offsets, 70.

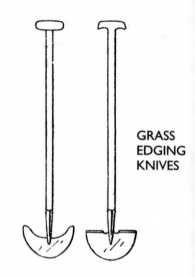

GRASS
EDGING
KNIVES

Fruit Garden.   Sever layered strawberries and replant on a new bed, 70.

Store apples, pears and plums, 69.

Grease-band fruit trees against winter moths, etc, 72.

Kitchen Garden.   Trap crane-fly grubs, 67.

Harvest spring onions. Sow onions for next year's crop.

Bend over tops of onions, 71.

Continue earthing celery, 71.

Lift second early potatoes.

Sow winter spinach, 72.

Feed leeks and thin carrots, 71.

Keep tomato side shoots nipped out. Expose fruits to sunshine, 71.

Pea and bean haulms should be removed and burned.

If cabbages are slow in hearting, give them a pinch of sulphate of ammonia.

Cut down globe artichokes, when the heads have been picked.

Under Glass.   Take chrysanthemum buds, 68.

Pot bulbs of Roman hyacinth, paper white narcissus and early daffodils.

Pot dwarf daffodils and irises to bloom in cold greenhouse.

Sow mignonette to bloom in warm house.

Pot up cinerarias and primulas.

Repot arum lilies which have been outside.

Take cuttings of ceanothus, aucubas, berberis and lavender.

Insert in cold frame, where they will soon root.

Paint greenhouse.

SEPTEMBER

Flower Garden. Make new lawns, 74.

Take cuttings of roses, 76.

Transplant seedling wallflowers, 79.

Lift and store gladioli.

Clear away exhausted annuals.

Tie up straggling border plants.

Anemones can be planted on light soils.

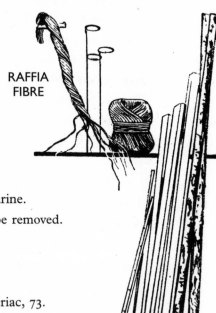

RAFFIA
FIBRE

STAKES

Fruit Garden. Plan new fruit garden. Order trees and bushes.

Prune black currant, raspberry, peach and nectarine.

Diseased leaves from strawberry plants should be removed.

Dress soil round blackcurrants, with manure.

Kitchen Garden. Lift and store carrots, marrows, onions and celeriac, 73.

Cut down the asparagus bed, 77.

Aid unripened tomatoes to completion and save seed, 77.

Lift and store main crop potatoes, 78. Lift and store beetroot, 78.

Protect cauliflowers, 78.

Earth-up celery finally, 80.

Lift leeks as required; hoe along rows, 80.

Harvest turnip crop and re-prepare bed to sow green top stone for turnip tops.

Cut down mint stalks and give a dressing of manure.

Commence blanching endive.

Thin out winter spinach.

Plant out cabbages for spring cutting.

Under Glass. Protect winter crops by cloches, 75.

Take cuttings of anchusa, geranium, phlox and viola, 76.

Lift and store begonias, 79.

Put pot plants in greenhouse.

Sow antirrhinums.

Put pot-grown chrysanthemums under glass to develop blooms.

Plant violets in frame.

GRAVEL RAKE

WOOD RAKE

Flower Garden. Dress lawns for worm trouble. Prick over and sprinkle fertiliser.

Sweep up leaves into heaps to rot down, 82.

Keep leaf-mould, sifted soil, sand, etc., under cover for potting.

Clear beds of summer flowers. Fork and manure where necessary.

Replant beds with bulbs and spring flowers.

Divide violas and replant 4 in. apart, 84.

Divide lupins and replant. Lift hollyhocks, cut and replant the young plants formed around the crown, 84.

Dress soil with bonemeal before replanting perennials.

Release and lift carnation layers. Replant new plants where needed.

Protect ranunculi with fibre, 85.

Protect pot chrysanthemums at night, and autumn-sown seedlings, 85.

Fruit Garden. Prepare sites for planting new fruit trees and bushes.

Prune currants, gooseberries and pear trees, 87.

Kitchen Garden. Lift parsnips if frost has touched them.

Blanche endive, 81.

BIRCH
BROOM

Sow mustard, rape, vetch or tares for green manuring, 81.

Protect seedlings of winter lettuce by frame or cloches.

Make a fresh compost heap, 83.

Plant rhubarb in a permanent position.

Set out spring greens, 86.

Make mushroom beds, 86. Examine vegetables in store, 86.

Heel broccoli over so that the heads face north.

Cut down old asparagus stems, and dress the bed with good rotted manure.

Under Glass. Protect bedding-plants and pot-plants with sheets of newspaper, 85.

Put chrysanthemums under glass at the end of the month. Those in pots go into the greenhouse, and border varieties in cold frame.

Clear hot-beds. Use the material for potting soil.

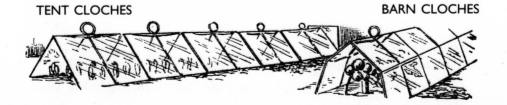

TENT CLOCHES   BARN CLOCHES

NOVEMBER

Flower Garden. Plant roses, 95.

Prepare and plant herbaceous border, 92.

Take cuttings of flowering shrubs, 92.

Plant May-flowering tulips, 96.

Top-dress lily-of-the-valley bed, 96.

Mulch rose trees with manure and rhododendrons with peat.

Divide clumps of hardy ferns.

Pack soil around primulas and auriculas.

Lift, dry and store montbretia bulbs in frost-free place.

PRUNING
KNIFE

Fruit Garden. Plant pear, plum and apple trees, 91.

Finish pruning and take cuttings of gooseberry and red currants, 94.

Spread manure between strawberry rows.

Apply basic slag to fruit trees after pruning.

Kitchen Garden. Dig and lime vacant plots.

Treat soil with a fumigant such as naphthalene to rid it of wireworm and lice.

Continue to clear ground of leaves. Use small ones for making leaf-mould.

Burn the bigger ones, 89.

Force seakale, 90.

Protect cabbage and support brussels sprouts, 90.

Force chicory and rhubarb, 92.

Plant Jerusalem artichokes and horse-radish.

Finish earthing up celery.

Earth up leeks.

Hoe between brussels, kale and cabbages.

Sow broad beans on light soil.

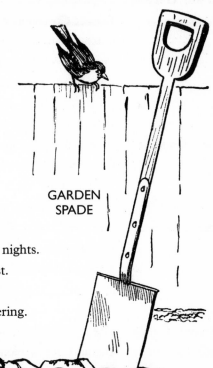

GARDEN
SPADE

Under Glass. Plant hyacinths, 96.

Pot lily-of-the-valley, 96.

Do not omit to cover plants with newspaper on frosty nights.

Give cinerarias enough water to keep soil slightly moist.

Keep the house dry and clean.

Cut down the chrysanthemums when they finish flowering.

Feed well-established cyclamens.

Prune grape vines.

DECEMBER

Flower Garden. Prepare new ground, 97.

Protect Christmas rose, 100.

Pinch out tops of wallflowers if growing too tall.

Plant leaf-losing shrubs, 103.

Renovate hedges and edgings, 103.

DOUBLE CUT PRUNER

Fruit Garden. Root-prune trees growing too vigorously at the expense of fruit.

Give fruit trees a winter spray, 104.

Winter-prune apple trees, 104.

Spray gooseberry bushes and protect them from birds, 104.

Limewash walls against which fruit trees grow.

Protect stone fruit, *i.e.* peaches, etc., with straw bands during severe weather.

Train and shape wall fruit trees.

Kitchen Garden. Plan the plot for the rotation of crops, 99.

Dig and trench plots, 102.

Earth up or cover crops against hard weather.

Make hot bed.

Prepare warm border for early sowings.

Wheel manure on plots when ground is frozen.

Potato sets for early planting can be exposed to light in sprouting boxes.

Under Glass.   Store bulbs in pots and boxes under greenhouse staging, 98.

Pack rhubarb and seakale in boxes with leaves and manure and cover them.

Keep old fuchsias dry, 98.

Cut down chrysanthemums with faded blooms to allow room for new shoots, 98.

Clean all flower-pots for future use, 98.

Examine stored roots. Destroy those decaying.

Cut out any slightly rotted parts on dahlia tubers. Dry and lime the cut parts, 100.

Give geranium cuttings just enough water to save them from drying out.

Stake freesias when they start to flower.

Hardy plants, such as primrose, polyanthus, forget-me-not and Solomon's seal, can be lifted and potted to supply early flowers.

A PAGE OF 'DO'S'

Burn all dead and diseased wood after pruning.

Transplant seedlings in the morning or evening, and not at midday.

Stake plants before the wind blows them down.

Plant roses firmly and spread their roots when doing so.

Cut away suckers directly they appear.

Pick off dead flowers; your border will have colour much longer.

Keep your eyes open for pests at all times, and deal with them accordingly.

Water cacti and greenhouse plants round the side of the pots, and not over them.

Remove weeds from the lawn directly they are seen.

Thin seedlings to the right distance apart, or your crops will suffer.

Keep the soil well hoed round onions, parsnips and carrots in the summer.

Pinch out side shoots of tomatoes immediately.

Keep greenhouse glass clean in winter.

Provide good stakes for fruit trees.

Wash all flower-pots before and after use.

Keep all tools clean and in good condition.

A PAGE OF 'DON'TS'

DON'T sow thickly or too deeply. The smaller the seed the shallower the sowing.

DON'T work on soil when it is very wet.

DON'T forget the undersides of leaves when spraying.

DON'T neglect to thin out seedlings.

DON'T neglect drainage or the soil will remain cold owing to constant evaporation.

DON'T dig at an oblique angle. Drive your spade down vertically.

DON'T omit liming. It helps organic decay and neutralizes acidity.

DON'T bury fertilisers too deeply or they will soon be wasted.

DON'T omit to soak ground before applying liquid fertilisers.

DON'T sprinkle water in dry weather. If you use water then give a soaking.

DON'T remove soil from roots of plants when transplanting.

DON'T use lime and farm manure at the same time.

DON'T use fresh soot; it should be weathered first.

DON'T use a dibber when planting bulbs; a trowel is better.

DON'T prune roses with frost about.

DON'T leave water lying on floor or staging in the greenhouse during the winter. Mop it up,

THREE TIPS FROM ADAM

Do not water seed-pans or pans of very small seedlings with a can. Instead, place the pan in a shallow bowl of water so that it seeps up through the soil. Watering with a can may disturb seeds, soil or seedlings. Let the pans drain for half an hour before placing in frame or on greenhouse staging.

Pot-plants which have been reached by frost should have the soil soaked with the coldest water you can get. Sprinkle foliage with the same cold water. Put the plants in a frost-proof shed. They will probably revive in a few hours. When unmistakable recovery has been made move them into warmth. Don't cut off any withered parts until a week after this treatment.

When making a circular bed or marking out circular drills use a board slightly longer than the circle radius. Make holes in it at required distances. Tapering pegs inserted in these are used as markers as the board is moved around on a stake driven through a hole at one end.

INDEX

Aconite, planting winter, 66
Alpines, how to grow, 19
American blight, 45
Anchusa, planting root cuttings, 76 Root
  cuttings, 59
Anemone, Japanese, root cuttings, 59
Annuals, 5
  Planting out half-hardy, raised under
    glass, 46
  Sowing, 65
Aphis, checking on rose trees, 49
  On fruit trees, 56
Apple, picking and storing, 69
Apple tree, best time for planting, 91
  Planting dwarf compact, 91
  Planting single cordon, 91
  Winter pruning, 104
Artificial fertiliser, how to use, 7
Asparagus, clearing beds, 77
  When and how to make bed, 38
Aucuba, 36
Azaleas, 54
Bark-ringing fruit trees, 45
Basket, how to fill a hanging, 40
  How to make a hanging, 40
  Plants suitable for a hanging, 40
Bed, making a circular, 142
Bed, flower-, diagrams of mixed spring,
  113; summer, 114
Beet, lifting, 78
Beet fly, 47
Beetroot, how to plant seedlings, 47
Begonia, how to start growth, 17
  Lifting and planting, 79
  Propagating by leaf cuttings, 59
Biennials, 5
Birds, protecting fruit bushes from, 104
Black currant, affected bushes, 62
Blight, spraying tomatoes, 61
Blind, 6
Brassicas, how to plant out, 47
Broad bean, 47
  How to sow, 21
Broccoli, how and when to grow, 39
Brussels sprouts, 47
  Care of, 90
  Planting out seedlings, 50
Cabbage, 47
  Main sowing of spring 64
Cactus, how to increase by cuttings, 42
Calceolaria, sowing, 51
Calendar month by month, 116–139
Calendula, sowing out of doors, 21

Canker, how to control on fruit trees, 20
Canna, how to sow in pots, 21
Canterbury bell, 13
Carnation, how to sow in pots, 21
  Layering, 60
Carrot, lifting the main crop, 73
  Outdoor sowing of early, 18
  Sowing early kinds for winter use, 47
  Sowing of early, 67
Cauliflower, 47
  Lifting, 78
Celeriac, how and when to grow, 39
  Lifting, storing, protecting, 73
Celery, care of, 62
  Earthing up, 71
  Outdoor planting of pot-grown, 53
  Preparing trenches, 22
  Protect during bad weather, 101
Chicory, forcing, 92
Chionodoxa, planting, 66, 70
Chives, how to grow, 33
Chrysanthemum, feeding, 68
  In pots under glass, 51
  Protect pot-plants from frost, 85
  Stimulating growth, 68
Clematis, how to plant, 36
  Root cuttings, 59
Cloche, use of, for supply of parsley, 75
Compost, 83
Colchicum, for rockery, 66, 70
Cold-frame, protecting plants from frost,
  9
  Preventing damage to plants, 85
Cornflower, sowing in drills, 65
Cosmos, planting out seedlings raised
  under glass, 46
Crane fly, 67
Cress, how to sow American and land for
  winter salads, 29
Crocus, planting, 66
Crown, 6
Cucumber, how to grow ridge, 41
Currant, Black, Red and White, 87
Cutting-back, 36
Cyclamen, repotting old corms of
  Persian, 66
Daffodil planting, 70
Dahlia, planting out pot-plants, 53
  Storing and planting, 24
Dandelion, forcing leaves for salads, 29
Dibber, how to make, 7
Don'ts on gardening, 141
Do's on gardening, 140

Dutch hoe, use of the, 55
Edgings, for garden paths, 103
Endive, blanching, 81
Eschscholtzia, sowing in drills, 65
Evergreen, clipping, 65
  Planting and clipping, 36
  Shoots as cuttings, 65
Feeding with liquid fertiliser, 55
Fennel, how to grow, 33
Ferns, repotting, 23
Fertiliser, how to use artificial, 7
Fertility, use of lime, 89
Flower-bed, diagrams for mixed, 114
  Diagrams for spring, 113
  Planting colour for a, 115
Frog-hopper, 47
Frost, pot-plant attacked by, 142
Protecting plants, 85
Fruit bush, feeding young, 20
Fruit tree, feeding young, 20
  How to control canker, 20
  Planting single, 93
Fuchsia, pruning of winter-stored, 17
Gadgets, adjustable drill-maker, 8
  Adjustable tool handle, 8
  Bed-maker, 8
  Earwig trap, 8
  Seed protector, 8
  Seedling drill-maker, 8
Garden, edgings for paths, 103
  Plan for a back garden, 107, 108, 109,
    110
  Plan for a front garden, 111, 112
  Planning a new, 105, 106
  Prepare soil for sowing and planting,
    102
Garden Line, 7
Geraniums, potting shoots, 76
Germination, use of glass to hasten, 75
Gladioli, lifting and storing, 79
  Planting, Sowing corms, 24
Glass to hasten germination, 75
Globe beet, sowing for autumn use, 67
Glory of the Snow. See Chionodoxa
Gloxinia, how to start growth, 17
Gooseberry, 87
  Planting, 95
  Pruning and planting cuttings, 95
Grafting, 35
Grass, sowing seed, 74
Green fly, checking on rose trees, 49
  On fruit trees, 56
Greengage, 69

Greenhouse, artificial heat, 98
  How to sow seeds in heated, 13
  Portable hanging shelves, 88
Green manuring, 81
Ground, avoid wasting space, 67
Half-hardy annuals, 5
Hanging basket, how to make, 40
Hardy annuals, 5
Hawthorn, planting, 103
Herbaceous, 5
  Border, preparing and planting, 92
Herbs, how and when to sow, 33
Holiday precautions, 63
Hollyhock, lifting and replanting, 84
Hot-bed, how to make, 10
Hover-fly, 49
Humus, leafmould, 6, 89
Hyacinth, indoor and outdoor, 96
Hydrangea, propagating, 55
Insecticide, the use of, 49
Iris, root cuttings, 59
Japanese anemone, root cuttings, 59
Kochia, how to sow in pots, 21
  Planting out seedlings raised under
    glass, 46
Kniphofia. See Red-hot poker
Kohl-rabi, when and how to sow, 37
Lacewing-fly, 49
Ladybird, 49
Land, preparation, sowing, planting, 102
Larkspur, sowing in drills, 65
Lateral, 6
Lawn, cutting out and laying new turf,
  74
  How to destroy daisies and plantains,
    53
  How to use lawn sand, 53
  Making good thin and bare patches, 68
Lawn mower, care of, 51
Leek, earthing up, 80
  Feeding, 71
  Planting out, 64
  Preparing ground, 22
Lettuce, catch crop, 50
  Planting out seedlings, 47
Lettuce, 16
  Winter sowing and planting, 81
Lily, how to plant *speciosum, tigrinum,
  regale* and *auratum*, 30
  Planting belladonna, 66
  Planting madonna, 66
Lily of the Valley, 96
  Lifting and replanting, 84

INDEX

Loam, 6
Lobelia, how to sow in pots, 21
Lupin, lifting and replanting, 84
Maize, how and when to plant, 50
Manure, green manuring, 81
    Home-made, 83
Manure pit, 82
Marigold, flowers and petals for salads, 67
Marrow, 54; storing vegetable, 73
Meadow saffron. See Colchicum
Michaelmas daisy, lifting and replanting, 84
Mildew, greenhouse tomatoes attacked by, 61
Mint, how to grow, 33
Mistletoe, growing seeds on trees, 98
Mower, lawn, care of, 56
Mulch, 6
    Grass clippings for a, 48
    How to apply, 58
Mushroom, grown out of doors, 86
    Growing in cellar or light-proof shed, 52. Planting the spawn, 52
    Preparing bed, 52
Mustard and cress, sowing of, 27
Narcissus, planting, 70
Nasturtium, leaves for salads, 67
Nemesia, planting out seedlings raised under glass, 46
Nigella, sowing in drills, 65
Offset, 6
Onion, checking growth, 71
    Hoeing, 50
    How to combat pests, 50
    How to produce good-sized, 18
    Lifting, 71
    Planting seedlings out of doors, 31
    Preparing bed for sets, 31
    Sowing of early, 18
    Stimulating growth by fertiliser, 31
Pæony, root cuttings, 59
Pampas grass, 85
Pansy cuttings, 55
Parsley, how to grow, 33
    Sowing, 64
Parsnip, sowing, 21
    Storing, 73
Pea, growing period of the sweet, 54
    How to obtain early, 16
    Planting out sweet, 34
    Preparing ground for green, 22
    Protecting from birds, 48

Sowing early, 21
Sowing sweet, 21
Pear, how to store, 69
Pear tree, best time for planting, 91
    Pruning, 87
Perennials, 5
Pests, checking winter, 72
    Cutworm, 12
    How to check wireworm, 12
    Millipedes, 12
    Rose mildew, 68
    Slugs, 12, 58. Snails, 12
Petunia, how to sow in pots, 21
Phlox, how to sow in pots, 21
    Root cuttings in pots, 76
Pink, propagating by pipings, 60
Plums, when ready for picking for storing and bottling, 69
Plum tree, best time for planting, 91
Potato, planting early, 26
Pot plants, attacked by frost, 142
    Care of, 48
    Repotting into larger pots, 25
Primrose, successive sowings of fairy, 50
Propagating bedding plants, 13
    Greenhouse plants by leaf cuttings, 59
Pruning, rose trees and bushes, 32
    Winter, 14
Radish, catch crop, 50
    Early sowings, 27
    Sowing, 64
Rain shelter for Alpines, 19
Raspberry, pruning, 62
Red currant planting, 95
Red-hot poker, 85
    Lifting and replanting, 84
Red spider, how to combat, 37
Rhododendron, 54
Rhubarb, forcing, 11, 92
    Leaves as spray for aphides, 67
    Lifting, 11
    Replanting, 11
Rock garden, how to construct, 15
    How to make a miniature, 28
    Plants on, 15
Rolling sawfly, 49
Root cuttings, 59
Rose, Christmas, protect from rain, 100
Rose mildew, how to check, 68
Rose sawfly grub, 49
Roses, budding standards, 57
    Disbudding standards, 48

Planting shoots of rambler, bush and climbing, 76
Planting trees, 95
Protecting trees from cold and wind, 9
Pruning ramblers, 65
Rambler shoots as cuttings, 65
When and how to prune, 32
Sage, how to grow, 33
Salads, first sowings, 27
    Protection against birds, 27
Salpiglossis, how to sow in pots, 21
    Planting out seedlings raised under glass, 46
Savory, how to grow, 33
Savoy, 47
Scabious, sowing in drills, 65
Seakale, forcing, 92
    How and when to grow, 37
    Indoor and outdoor forcing of roots, 90
Seed-box, made of zinc, 88
Seedlings, stopping 'damping off,' 34
    How to water, 142
    Protection from birds, 26
    Transplanting into boxes, 34
Seeds, sowing, 13
Shallots, 71
    Planting, 26
    When ready for lifting, 64
Shrub, planting evergreen, 103
    Planting shoots from flowering, 92
Small garden, types of fruit trees, 93
Snowdrop planting, 66
Soil, keeping it moist, 58
Soot, used as a fertiliser, 88
Spinach, 67
    Preparing soil for winter, 72
    Sowing, 21
Spit, 6
Spraying winter fruit trees, 104
Spring bed, diagrams for flower, 113
Spring greens, planting, 86
Squill, planting, 66
Staking, 46
Stock, how to sow ten-week in pots, 21
Storage, checking, 86
Storing, examine roots and tubers, 100
    In greenhouse, 93
Strawberry layering, 60
    Transplant layered runners, 70
Stripe, greenhouse tomatoes attacked by, 61
Subsoil, 6

Succulent plants from seeds, 42
Suckers, 6
Summer bed, diagrams of mixed flower, 115
Sweet pea, growing period, 54
    Planting out, 34
    Sowing, 21
Sweet William, 13
Taking the bud, 6
Tap-root, 6
Tarragon, how to grow, 33
Thyme, how to grow, 33
Tidying up, 82
Tilth, 6
Tobacco flower, how to sow in pots, 21
Tools, cleaning and sharpening, 100
    Old fork and spade handles, 101
Tomato, 56
    Diseases, 61
    How to cultivate, 43
    Ripening, 77
    Saving seeds, 77
    Storing maincrop, 78
Transplanting early spring plants, 13
Tulips, planting Darwin and cottage, 90
    Treatment of, 46
Turnip, harvesting, 80
    Preparing bed, 80
Vegetable, change of beds, 99
    Continuous supply, 75
    Grown in same soil, 99
    Sowing in same plot, 99
    Underfeeding of soil, 99
Vine, growing under glass, 51
Viola cuttings, 55
    Lifting and replanting, 84
    Planting non-flowering shoots, 76
Violet, beds in cold frames, 101
Wall, sloping, suitable for Alpine plants, 19
Wallflower, 13
    Transplanting seedlings, 79
Waste, use of, 6
Watercress, cultivation in garden, 29
Watering, 58
Weeding, 34
Weevil, how to combat the strawberry, 37
Window-box, how to make, 44
    Plants suitable, 44
Winter spraying, fruit trees, 104
Wireworms, 56
Woolly aphis, 45
Wormcast on lawns, 92